The Oryx Multicultural Folktale Series

Cinderella

by
Judy Sierra

Illustrated by
Joanne Caroselli

ORYX PRESS
1992

398
c

The rare Arabian Oryx is believed to have inspired the myth of the unicorn. This desert antelope became virtually extinct in the early 1960s. At that time several groups of international conservationists arranged to have 9 animals sent to the Phoenix Zoo to be the nucleus of a captive breeding herd. Today the Oryx population is nearly 800, and over 400 have been returned to reserves in the Middle East.

Library of Congress Cataloging-in-Publication Data

Sierra, Judy.
    The Oryx multicultural folktale series : Cinderella / by Judy
Sierra.
        p. cm.
    Includes bibliographical references and index.
    Summary: Presents versions of the Cinderella story which represent many cultures, geographical areas, and styles. Includes information about the tales, related activities, and resources.
    ISBN 0-89774-727-5
    1. Fairy tales. 2. Cinderella (Tale) [1. Fairy tales.
2. Cinderella (Tale) 3. Folklore.] I. Title.
PZ8.S34560r 1992
398.21—dc20   92-16476
                                                       CIP
                                                       AC

Contents

Preface

The tales in this book are presented for the enjoyment of anyone who would like to explore the mystery of how a folktale may vary as it is told in different cultures and in different times. The tales known collectively as Cinderella stories are perhaps the most widely recorded of all traditional narratives. Now considered a children's story, and censored to fit adult ideas of what is and is not suitable for children, tales of Cinderella and her cousins were once told by adults for all members of the community. The evils that befell the heroine in oral tales were frightening, even gruesome. But she survived unharmed and triumphant, with the help of strange and magical beings much more mysterious and powerful than Disney's helpful birds and sweet fairy godmother.

In 1893, the English Folklore Society published Marian Roalfe Cox's *Cinderella: Three Hundred and Forty-Five Variants of Cinderella, Catskin, and Cap o' Rushes, Abstracted and Tabulated, with a Discussion of Medieval Analogues and Notes.* This was the first study of what seemed to be different versions of the same folktale. Since the publication of Cox's book, many other Cinderella stories have been collected and published. From them, I have chosen twenty-four that represent a broad range of cultures and geographical areas, styles, and variations on the basic theme of the persecuted heroine. I have selected versions that have a coherent and interesting plot—many orally collected texts seem fragmented, or contain elements that do not make sense in a contemporary context, though they are, of course, valuable to scholars. I particularly looked for stories that can be appreciated by young readers, while avoiding the many watered-down retellings. I have tried to be as true as possible to early written versions of tales, though in a few cases (as explained in the tale notes), I have made minor alterations for the sake of sense, and in two instances combined elements from closely related texts. I have included in the notes to the tale as much infor-mation as I have been able to find about the circumstances of the collecting of the tale and of the editorial methods of the compiler. Most compilers, from the Grimms to Richard Chase, freely admit to combining various versions of a tale and adding their own touches to make the tales better to read. The telling of folktales usually took place within small, familiar groups, and a word-for-word recording of a telling would not be able to convey important parts of the story expressed through gesture and facial expression, or which were left unstated because of the common knowledge of the group. Words must be added to make up for this lack.

The study of folktales raises many more questions than there are answers. Where and how were these tales first told? What was the meaning of those strange happenings, those magical creatures, to the people who first told the tales? Were they as mysterious to them as they are to us today? Scholars have only come up with tentative answers to these questions. Perhaps some of the young people reading these tales now for the first time will devise new ways of studying them. I have included information about the tales both in brief introductory notes and in more complete notes in a section following the tales. Unfortunately, more is known about some tales, collectors, storytellers, and storytelling traditions than others, thus some of these notes are unavoidably sketchy.

The following introduction, and the notes preceding each tale, are written to be read aloud to children as young as six and alone by those nine and up. The delight of these tales, as well as the challenge of comparing two or more versions, knows no age limit.

For the teacher, I have suggested a range of related activities from drama and creative writing to critical comparison of picture book editions. I have also included a bibliography of picture book retellings of Cinderella tales, a finding guide to tale variants in collections, and a list of recommended further readings on Cinderella tales.

Acknowledgments

In compiling this anthology, I am very much indebted to Marian Roalfe Cox, who in 1893 published summaries of 345 Cinderella tales which she collected from books, journals, and national archives. Her work allowed me in many cases to locate and work with early written versions of Cinderella stories. The faculty of the Folklore and Mythology Program at UCLA, and especially Donald Ward, introduced me to the scholarly study of folktales and storytelling. And I owe great and heartfelt thanks to Howard Batchelor of The Oryx Press, who saw in my idea not just a book, but a series.

Acknowledgments to Contributors

Grateful acknowledgment is made to the following for permission to reprint their copyrighted material. Every reasonable effort has been made to trace the ownership of all copyrighted stories in this volume. Any errors that may have occurred are inadvertent and will be corrected in subsequent editions, provided notification is sent to the publisher. Stories not listed are assumed to be in the public domain.

Inea Bushnaq. "The Little Red Fish and the Clog of Gold" from *Arab Folktales* by Inea Bushnaq. Copyright © 1986 by Inea Bushnaq. Reprinted by permission of Pantheon Books, a division of Random House, Inc.

Richard Chase. "Ashpet" from *The Grandfather Tales* by Richard Chase. Copyright © 1948 by Richard Chase. Copyright renewed 1976 by Richard Chase. Reprinted by permission of Houghton Mifflin Co.

Genevieve Massignon. "Peu d'Anisso" from *Folktales from France* edited by Genevieve Massignon and translated by Jacqueline Hyland. Copyright © 1968 by University of Chicago Press. Reprinted by permission of University of Chicago Press.

Phumla M'bane. "Nomi and the Magic Fish" from *Nomi and the Magic Fish: A Story from Africa* by Phumla M'bane. Copyright © 1972 by Doubleday. Used by permission of Doubleday, a division of Bantam Doubleday Dell Publishing Group, Inc.

Keiko Seki. "Benizara and Kakezara" from *Folktales of Japan* edited by Keiko Seki and translated by Robert J. Adams. Copyright © 1963 by University of Chicago Press. Reprinted by permission of University of Chicago Press.

"Yeh-hsien" from "The Chinese Cinderella Story" by Arthur Waley in *Folk-Lore* 58 (1947): 226-38. Adapted by Judy Sierra. Adapted with permission of the Folklore Society (Great Britain).

Tales

Introduction to the Tales

The stories in this book were first told long ago and were told over and over in times and places where there were no books or writing (and, of course, no movies or television), until they were written down by "collectors" of folktales. Cinderella stories can be found in more parts of the world, told in more languages, and in more different ways than any other folktale. A young girl (or sometimes a boy) is mistreated by her family, but she receives magical help so that she can be recognized for the good and beautiful person that she really is. There are hundreds of ways of telling this story. For instance, there are different terrible jobs or impossible tasks that the girl's cruel family gives her; there are all sorts of magical people and animals that help her; and there are many surprising ways in which a prince or a king recognizes her true identity. Yet somehow the basic story remains the same, a story very much like the one we know as "Cinderella."

We can understand the way folktales are learned and passed on by word of mouth by looking at our own oral traditions. But wait! If you can read this book, you obviously know how to read and write. So how could *you* have an oral tradition? Think about the stories, songs, jokes, and sayings you know that you didn't learn from a book:

- How many ghost stories can you tell?
- How many knock-knock jokes do you know?
- How many songs can you sing about school and teachers that you wouldn't want your teacher to hear?
- How many jump rope rhymes can you repeat?
- How many rhymes for hand-clapping games do you know?

If you do know some of these, and you didn't learn them from a book, then you're part of an oral tradition yourself. You probably heard these stories, jokes, songs, and rhymes twice, three times, or more before you really knew them. This is how storytelling works in an oral tradition. Some folktales are very long—perhaps a whole night or more in the telling. People hear them over and over, beginning when they are very young. Those who like telling the tales and have a knack for making them seem new and exciting every time become storytellers.

Jump-rope rhymes and hand-clapping games show how the oral tradition changes and still stays basically the same. Have you ever met someone who knows a jump-rope rhyme (maybe one that starts, "Cinderella, dressed in yella. . .") just a little differently than you, or who adds a different ending to it? Or someone who uses the same rhymes for a hand-clapping game with a few words changed? Somehow, people change the words in folk rhymes and folktales without planning to. The words just come out differently. If the people who hear them like the new words, this new version will catch on and be repeated. Then, someone else will make newer, better changes—or go back to the first version. Small changes happen all the time, but something important—the skeleton, the framework, the rules—stays the same.

So it is and was with folktales. Does this mean that the tale of Cinderella was first told in just one place and then people told it to each other until it changed and spread all across the world, like gossip? Or, did many different people in different places simply make up stories that were alike? Folklorists—the women and men who study such things as folktales—have been arguing about this very question for over a hundred years, and there just doesn't seem to be a way of explaining why a story like Cinderella is found far and wide, always the same yet always different.

Most likely, if you ask a friend to tell you the story of Cinderella, he or she will talk about the Walt Disney movie. A child as young as five or six years old can often tell the whole story of Cinderella from beginning to end. If you have the patience to listen to such a retelling, you will get an idea of how memory for folktales works. The story will be Cinderella, without a doubt, yet each storyteller will emphasize different parts and skip others, and may even invent things that were not in the movie. Try asking one of your grandparents, great-grandparents, or another older friend or relative if they can tell you a story that's like Cinderella. If you're lucky, you may discover still another version of this ancient tale!

The first Cinderella story to be written down, in around the year 850 A.D., was the Chinese tale of Yeh-hsien. Even earlier, nearly two thousand years ago, a Greek writer told of an Egyptian king who searched for the unknown owner of a beautiful sandal. Neither of these seem like the fairy tales we are used to reading in books, but they give us an idea of how old and how widespread Cinderella tales really are.

Rhodopis

Strabo, a Greek historian who lived around the time of the birth of Christ, recorded a story told in Egypt about Rhodopis, a woman buried, so it was said, in one of the great pyramids. Rhodopis was bathing one day when an eagle swooped down and grabbed one of her sandals from the hands of a female servant. The eagle flew off to the Egyptian city of Memphis and dropped the sandal into the lap of the king. The king was fascinated with the size and shape of this sandal, and so he sent messengers throughout the country to find its owner. They found Rhodopis in the city of Naucratis and brought her to the king, who married her.

Strabo tells this story as history, not fairy tale, and we don't know if Rhodopis was in any other way a Cinderella. Did she have a wicked stepmother, for example? This is the earliest written record we have of a unique motif of the Cinderella story, the slipper test for choosing a bride.

Yeh-hsien

The first complete Cinderella story to be written down, over one thousand years ago, comes from China. It tells of Yeh-hsien, a girl who was mistreated by her stepmother and stepsister after her father remarried. Like the heroines of several other Cinderella tales, Yeh-hsien was helped by a magical talking fish. Many parts of the story remain a mystery—we do not know exactly what a *cave-master* did, or where the land of *T'o-han* was, or whether the Tomb of the Two Women really existed. The tale is brief, more like an outline or summary than a real story, yet it is difficult to forget.

Among the people of the south there is a tradition that before the Ch'in and Han dynasties there lived a cave-master called Wu. People called the place the Wu cave. He had two wives. One wife died. She had a daughter called Yeh-hsien, who from childhood was intelligent and good at making pottery on the wheel. Her father loved her. After some years the father died, and she was ill-treated by her stepmother, who would always order her to collect firewood in dangerous places and draw water from deep pools. Once Yeh-hsein caught a fish about two inches long, with red fins and golden eyes. She put it into a bowl of water. It grew bigger every day, and after she had changed the bowl several times, she could find no bowl big enough for it, so she threw it back into the pond. Whatever food was left over from meals she put into the water to feed it. When Yeh-hsien came to the pond, the fish always swam up and rested its head on the bank, but when anyone else came, it would not come out.

The stepmother watched for the fish, but it did not once appear. So she tricked the girl, saying, "Haven't you worked hard! I am going to give you a new dress." She then made the girl change out of her tattered clothing. Afterwards she sent her to get water from a spring that was very far away. The stepmother put on Yeh-hsien's clothes, hid a sharp knife up her sleeve, and went to the pond. She called to the fish. The fish at once put its head out, and she chopped it off and killed it. The fish was now more than ten feet long. She cooked it, and when she served it up, it tasted twice as good as an ordinary fish. She hid the bones under the dung-hill.

The next day, when the girl came to the pond, no fish appeared. The girl ran out into the fields, howling with grief. Suddenly there appeared a man with his hair loose over his shoulders, dressed in coarse clothes. He descended from the sky, and he consoled her, saying, "Don't cry so! Your stepmother has killed the fish and its bones are under the dung-heap. Go back, take the fish's bones and hide them in your room. Whatever you want, you have only to ask the fish bones for it." The girl followed his advice, and from then on she was able to provide herself with gold, pearls, dresses, and food whenever she wanted them.

When the time came for the cave festival, the stepmother took her own daughter with her, and left Yeh-hsien to keep watch over the fruit trees in the garden. The girl waited until they were far away, and then she followed them, wearing a cloak of material spun from kingfisher feathers and shoes of gold. Her stepsister saw her and said to the stepmother, "That girl looks like my sister." The stepmother suspected the same thing. The girl was aware of this and went away in such a hurry that she lost one shoe. It was picked up by one of the people of the cave. When the stepmother got home, she found the girl asleep, with her arms round one of the trees in the garden, and thought no more about it.

The cave was near an island in the sea, and on this island was a kingdom called T'o-han. The man who had picked up the gold shoe sold it in T'o-han, and it was brought to the king. He ordered all the women of the court to put it on, but it was too small even for the one among them that had the smallest foot. He then ordered all the women in his kingdom to try it on, but there was not one that it fitted. It was as light as down, and it made no noise even when treading on stone. His search finally took him to the place where Yeh-hsien lived with her stepmother, and the shoe fitted her perfectly. She put on the other shoe, and her cape of feathers, and she was as beautiful as a heavenly being. Taking the fish bones with her, she returned with the king to T'o-han and became his chief wife. The first year, the king was very greedy and asked the fish bones for jade and pearls without limit. The next year, the fish bones no longer granted his requests. He buried them by the sea shore and covered them with a hundred bushels of pearls, and after a while they were washed away by the tide.

The stepmother and stepsister were struck by flying rocks, and died. The cave people buried them in a stone pit, which was called the Tomb of the Two Women. Men would come there and make offerings, and the girl they prayed for would become their wife.

Cinderella,
or the Little Glass Slipper

*T*he French author Charles Perrault published Cinderella (*Cendrillon* in French) in 1697, in a collection of fairy tales. This is the story most people recognize as the *real* Cinderella. Walt Disney's animated film is based on Perrault. However, only a few of the hundreds of other Cinderella tales recorded include a glass slipper (it is more often gold), or a fairy godmother, or a pumpkin carriage, or a warning to come home before midnight.

Perrault was a member of the royal court of Louis XIV of France at Versailles, and the clothing he describes was the very latest French fashion of the time. King Louis himself wore a long curly wig, breeches, stockings, and high-heeled shoes. He probably would have wanted the glass slipper for himself.

*O*nce upon a time, a gentleman took a second wife. She was the proudest and haughtiest woman ever there was, and she had two daughters who were like her in every way. And the man had a young daughter of his own, but she was without equal in sweetness and goodness. In this, she took after her mother, who had been the nicest person in the world.

Their wedding was scarcely over when the stepmother's evil temper erupted. She couldn't bear the girl's good nature, which made her own daughters seem even more hateful. She heaped upon her the dirtiest housework—it was she who washed the dishes and scrubbed the stairs, who swept Madame's room and that of The Young Ladies, her daughters. She slept in the attic on a dirty mattress, while her sisters stayed in rooms with parquet floors, fashionable beds, and mirrors that showed them from head to toe. The poor girl endured all this patiently and dared not complain to her father. He would have scolded her, for he always did what his wife told him.

When her work was done, she would go to the fireplace and sit in the ashes, and for this reason, everyone called her Cinderbottom. Her younger stepsister, who was not as spiteful as the elder, called her Cinderella. Nonetheless, Cinderella, for all her nasty clothes, was still a hundred times more beautiful than her sisters, no matter how magnificently they dressed.

And it happened that the king's son gave a ball and invited all the finer folks. Our Two Young Ladies were invited, for they had quite a reputation around about. Picture them pleased and busy deciding which clothes and hair styles would suit them best. New work for Cinderella, for it was she who ironed their linen and made tiny little pleats in their ruffles. They talked of nothing but what they would wear.

"I," said the elder, "shall wear my red velvet dress and my English lace."

"I," said the younger, "only have last year's skirt. But I shall make up for that by wearing my coat with the gold flowers and my diamond jewelry, which is not at all unfashionable."

The hairdresser was called in to make their hair into the latest style, and expensive trimmings were bought from the best designers. They called Cinderella to ask her opinion, since she always had good taste. Cinderella gave them only the best advice, and even offered to help arrange their hair, to which they agreed gladly.

As she helped her stepsisters, they asked her, "Cinderella, don't *you* want to go to the ball?"

"Oh dear, ladies, you are making fun of me. It wouldn't be right."

"That's true," they giggled. "People would surely laugh to see a Cinderbottom at the ball!"

Hearing such insults, any other sister would have made those two look as ugly as possible, but Cinderella was good-hearted and worked to make them look pretty. They didn't eat a bite for almost two days, they were so excited. They broke more than a dozen laces while pulling their corsets as tight as possible, and they were *always* standing in front of their mirror.

At last the happy day arrived. The sisters left, and Cinderella followed them with her eyes as long as she could. When she could see them no longer, she started to cry.

Her godmother saw her in tears and asked her what was wrong.

"I wish . . . I wish . . ." But she was crying so hard, she couldn't finish.

Her godmother, who was a fairy, said to her, "You would like to go to the ball, wouldn't you?"

"Oh, yes," sighed Cinderella.

"Very well, will you be a good girl? Then I'll arrange it," said her godmother. She led Cinderella into her room and said, "Go to the garden and bring me a pumpkin."

Cinderella went at once and picked the prettiest one she could find, and carried it to her godmother, though she couldn't guess how that pumpkin could help her go to the ball. The godmother hollowed out the pumpkin, leaving only the shell, struck it with her wand, and the pumpkin was instantly changed into a beautiful golden carriage.

Afterwards, the godmother went and looked in the mousetrap, where she found six lively mice. She told Cinderella to lift the door of the trap a bit, then she touched each mouse with her wand as it ran out, and instantly the mice changed into beautiful horses. They made a fine team of six, harnessed to the carriage, each with a lovely coat of dappled mouse-grey.

But the godmother couldn't decide what to use to make a coachman.

"I'll go see if there isn't a rat in the rat-trap," said Cinderella.

"Good thinking," said her godmother, "go and look."

Cinderella brought her the trap, with three fat rats inside. The fairy chose one of the three, on account of his fabulous whiskers, and when she touched him, he turned into a fat coachman, with the handsomest mustache ever seen.

"Now go into the garden," she told Cinderella. "Behind the watering pot you will find six lizards. Bring them to me."

She had no sooner brought them than her godmother transformed them into six footmen who jumped quickly onto the back of the carriage in their fancy uniforms and held on as if they had never done otherwise in all their lives.

Then her godmother said, "Well, here is all you need to go to the ball. Are you happy?"

"Yes . . . but am I going like this in my old ugly clothes?"

Her godmother just touched her with the wand and instantly her clothes were changed into cloth of silver and gold, embroidered with jewels. And then she gave Cinderella a pair of glass slippers, the loveliest in the world. Thus bedecked, Cinderella climbed aboard the coach. Above all else, her godmother told her, she must not stay out past midnight. If she stayed at the ball even one second longer, the coach would change back into a pumpkin, her horses into mice, her footmen into lizards, and her clothes into the old dirty rags she had worn before.

Cinderella promised her godmother that she wouldn't fail to leave the ball before midnight, and she rode off in her coach, her heart filled with joy.

When the king's son was told of the arrival of a mysterious princess, he hurried to welcome her. He gave Cinderella his hand as she stepped down from the coach, and he led her into the hall where all the guests were assembled. A hush fell over them all. The dancing stopped and the violins fell silent as everyone watched her. "Oh, how lovely she is," everyone seemed to whisper.

The king himself, old though he was, couldn't take his eyes off her. He said to the queen that he had not seen such a beautiful and charming person in years. All the ladies paid close attention to her clothes, so that the next day they could copy them—if only they could find the right fabric and seamstresses clever enough to make them.

The king's son asked Cinderella to take the seat of honor, and afterward he asked her to dance. She danced so gracefully that everyone admired her even more.

A sumptuous feast was brought in, but the young prince could not eat. He could only stare at Cinderella. She went and sat beside her sisters, and spoke to them most politely. She even shared with them the oranges and lemons that the king had given her. Her kindness surprised the two sisters, for they did not know who she was.

As they were talking, Cinderella heard the clock strike a quarter to twelve. She quickly made a deep curtsy to them all and ran out as fast as she could. She found her godmother waiting for her at home, and after thanking her, she told her how much she wished she could go to the ball again the following night, for the king's son had invited her. And as she was busy telling her godmother everything that had happened, the two sisters knocked at the door. Cinderella went to open it for them.

"You've been gone so long," she said to them, yawning and rubbing her eyes and stretching as if she had just awakened. In truth, she hadn't been the least bit tired since she had last seen them.

"If you had been at the ball," one of her sisters said, "you wouldn't have been bored. A princess came—the most beautiful ever seen—and she was uncommonly friendly with us and gave us oranges and lemons."

Cinderella pretended to be enthralled. She asked the name of the princess, but her stepsisters answered that they did not know. The king's son was suffering, they said, and would give anything to know who she was. Cinderella smiled and said, "So, she was very pretty? You are so lucky. Is there any way I could see her? Please, Mademoiselle Javotte, lend me your plain yellow dress."

"Really!" said Mademoiselle Javotte. "The very idea! I'd have to be crazy to lend my dress to a nasty Cinderbottom like you."

Cinderella had expected this answer, and this was fine with her—she wouldn't have known what to do if her sister *had* wanted to lend her the dress.

The following day, the two sisters went to the ball, and Cinderella went also, but dressed even more splendidly than the first time. The king's son stuck close to her and paid her endless compliments, and Cinderella was enjoying herself so much, she forgot her godmother's warning. She could have sworn it was only eleven when she heard the first stroke of midnight. She rose and fled as swiftly as a fawn. The prince ran after her, but he couldn't catch her. She let fall one of her glass slippers, which the prince carefully picked up.

Cinderella arrived home out of breath, without coach or lackeys, wearing her old, ugly clothes. Nothing remained of her magnificence except one small slipper, the mate of the one she had dropped. The guards of the palace gate were asked if they had seen anyone leave. They said they had seen no one, except a shabbily dressed young girl who looked more like a poor country lass than a fine lady.

When her two sisters returned from the ball, Cinderella asked them if they had enjoyed themselves this time and if the beautiful lady had been there. They told her that she had, but that she had run away when the clock struck midnight, and so hastily that she had dropped one of her glass slippers—the loveliest in the world. The king's son had picked it up and had done nothing but look at it the rest of the night. Surely he was completely in love with the beautiful owner of the little slipper.

They spoke the truth, for several days later, the king's son announced that he would marry the young lady whose foot fit the glass slipper. They tried it first on the princesses, then the duchesses, then everyone at court, but in vain. They brought it to the house of the two sisters, who did everything possible to make their feet squeeze into the slipper, but they couldn't do it.

Cinderella watched all this. "Let's see if it doesn't fit me," she said.

Her sisters laughed out loud at this. The gentleman who held the slipper, having looked closely at Cinderella and found her quite lovely, said that was only fair, and that he had been ordered to try it on all the young women. He made Cinderella sit down, and trying the slipper, he saw that it fit easily, as if it were a wax mold of her foot. Her two sisters were shocked, but even more so when Cinderella drew another little slipper from her pocket and put it on her other foot. Just then her godmother arrived, and touching Cinderella's clothes with her wand, caused them to become even more magnificent than before.

Then her two sisters knew she was the beautiful person that they had seen at the ball. They threw themselves at her feet to ask her forgiveness for the way they had made her suffer. Cinderella ordered them to rise, and embraced them, and forgave them with all her heart, and asked them to be her friends. She was taken to the young prince, dressed in her new finery. He found her lovelier than ever, and a few days afterward they were married. Cinderella, who was as good as she was beautiful, brought her sisters to live at the palace and married them the same day to two great lords of the court.

Moral
For a maiden, beauty is a rare treasure,
Which one never tires of admiring.
But what we call grace
Is without price, and worth far more.
This is what Cinderella's godmother gave her,
Instructing her so well that she made a queen of her.

(So says the moral of this story)
Fair ones, this gift is greater than beauty.
In the end, in order to win someone's heart,
Graciousness is the true fairies' gift.
Without it, one can do nothing;
With it, one can do anything!

Another Moral
It is surely a great advantage
To have intelligence and daring,
Good breeding and good sense,
And other such qualities
Which one receives from on high!
Even though you have these,
You will not have success,
Unless, to make them count, you have
A godfather or a godmother.

Peu d'Anisso

The heroine of Perrault's Cinderella has trouble with her stepmother, but in another kind of Cinderella tale the heroine has trouble with her father. Her mother is dead, and her father has promised to remarry only if he finds another wife as beautiful as she. As his daughter grows up, she begins to look more and more like her mother, and her father decides to marry *her*. The girl runs away from home after tricking her father into giving her three beautiful dresses. The prince in this tale is certainly not very charming; he never apologizes to Peu d'Anisso for his rudeness.

This story was told by a traditional French storyteller in 1960.

*T*here was a gentleman who had a very beautiful wife. His wife said to him before she died, "Do not marry again unless you find a woman as beautiful as I am."

When the gentleman became a widower, he looked everywhere for a wife as beautiful as his first, but he could not find one.

This gentleman had a daughter. As she grew older, she looked much like her mother, so the father wanted to marry her. The girl would not listen to her father. She went to find her godmother, who was a *fado*—a fairy—and who said to her, "Before you decide, ask your father for the most beautiful dresses in the whole world and wait and see what he does."

The father had people hunting everywhere for the dresses his daughter longed for, but the more she had, the more she asked for. In the end he said to her, "You'll bring me to ruin!" Still he pressed his suit.

The girl went to her godmother again, who said to her, "You are to run away from your father. I shall give you a chest, which goes underground, and a wand to make it do your bidding. You shall hide under a *peu d'anisso*, a she-donkey's skin, bringing the ears down over your face, and you'll leave your father's home."

The girl took the wand and the chest. When she said to the chest, "Open up!" the chest opened, and she put her lovely dresses into it.

She dressed herself in rags, and hiding under the she-donkey's skin, she fled during the night.

The next day she showed up at the king's farm. She was hired as a turkey girl.

She looked so poor and dirty under her she-donkey's skin that at first she was left to sleep outside with her turkeys. Poor Peu d'Anisso! The turkeys came and rubbed against her, and this made her even more dirty. The Prince used to watch her going by and teased her because she looked so poor and so dirty.

When she was asked her name, she just replied, "I'm called Peu d'Anisso."

"*Peu d'Anisso*? What a gorgeous name for a turkey girl!"

The owner of the farm asked her, "What can you do while you look after your turkeys? Do you know how to sew or how to knit?"

Peu d'Anisso answered, "I know how to make lace." Now this was true. Peu d'Anisso made the most beautiful lace in the world. Seeing that she worked so well, the owner of the farm gave her a room to sleep in. Then Peu d'Anisso took her chest and touched it with her wand, saying, "Open up!"

The chest opened. All the lovely dresses were there, and every evening Peu d'Anisso would wash and comb her hair and try on one of her dresses.

One winter's day Peu d'Anisso was keeping warm in a corner of the hearth. The prince went by there, and he picked up a poker and gave her a poke with it to keep her at arm's length.

The next day there was a big ball in that part of the country. The king's son went to it, like everybody else. When everyone had left, Peu d'Anisso came into her room and opened her chest and took out one of her loveliest dresses. Then she ordered her chest to lead her underground to where the ball was being given. As she came in, everyone stared at her. The king's son went over to fetch her to dance with him. When the dance was over, he asked her her name.

"I'm called 'Poker-Poke.'"

"Ah-ha!" said the king's son. "Poker-Poke is a good name. I'll remember that, all right!"

The next day the king's son called at the farm and talked of the ball and the lovely girl who had been there. He started to tell them, "I danced with the most beautiful girl I have ever seen . . ."

"No more beautiful than I! No more fair!" Peu d'Anisso began saying as she warmed her ragged clothing by the fire.

"Shut up, Peu d'Anisso!" said the king's son, teasing her, and he took the bellows and gave her a puff from them to shame her.

A little later on, another ball was being held. The same thing happened. The king's son begged the beautiful girl to come and dance with him. She had an even more gorgeous dress on and she looked so lovely.

"What is your name?"

"I am called Bellows-Puff."

"Ah! Bellows-Puff is a good name. I'll remember that, all right!"

The next day he found himself once more with Peu d'Anisso, and he talked of his meeting this beautiful girl again.

"No more beautiful than I, no more fair!" she said very softly as she stirred up the ashes in the hearth.

"Shut up, Peu d'Anisso!" said the king's son, who was irritated by all this. He picked up a *friquet*—a stick—and struck Peu d'Anisso with it.

Not long after, there was another ball given. The king's son met the lovely girl again. She was wearing yet another dress. He asked her her name.

"I'm called Friquet-stick."

"Ah-ha! Friquet-stick is a good name. I'll remember that, all right."

Without being any the wiser, the king's son went home while Peu d'Anisso, thanks to her chest, fled underground.

Some time later the king's son fell ill. He took to his bed because he was so sick with worry. By constantly thinking of the pretty girl's name, he had got to the stage of asking himself whether she had anything to do with Peu d'Anisso. Had she not said to him, "No more beautiful than I, no more fair . . ."? He was so sick with worry that he refused to eat any of the food brought to him. One fine day he said, "I don't want to eat anything but soup made by Peu d'Anisso."

"Oh, poor Peu d'Anisso! Surely you won't ask *her* to make you a soup?"

"I will eat only soup made by Peu d'Anisso."

The turkey girl was asked to make the soup for the king's son. She washed herself and combed her hair and put on one of her loveliest dresses so as to be clean to make this soup. The king's son got up without anyone knowing and looked through the keyhole. He saw the beautiful dresses spread all over the room. They shone like gold. As for the girl, she was surely the one he had seen at the ball.

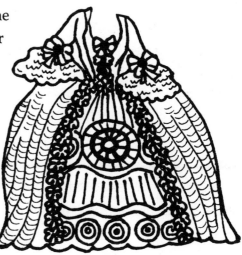

"Open up! Open up, Peu d'Anisso!" he cried.

The girl opened the door, but she never again wore her donkey skin because the king's son did not want her to. I don't know whether he ate the soup made by Peu d'Anisso, but what is certain is that he married her and they both were very happy.

Aschenputtel

*A*schenputtel is an old German word for a little pot that sits in the fireplace. The heroines of many Cinderella tales sit or sleep in the ashes. When reading these stories, it is important to realize that in other times and places the fireplace or hearth was often quite large and was used for heating and for cooking meals.

This tale and the following two are from the famous German folktale collection of Jacob and Wilhelm Grimm. Aschenputtel's stepsisters try to make the slipper fit them by cutting off parts of their feet. This gruesome detail is included in many other versions of Cinderella. Other elements found in this tale, but not in Perrault's Cinderella, are the magic tree on the mother's grave and the impossible task of picking up thousands of tiny grains.

*O*nce upon a time there was a rich man whose wife lay sick, and when she felt her end drawing near, she called her only daughter to her bedside, and said,

"Beloved child, be good, and have faith, and God will always take care of you, and I will look down upon you from heaven, and will be with you."

And with these words she closed her eyes and died.

The girl visited her mother's grave each day and wept, and she was always good and faithful. When winter came, the snow spread a white blanket upon the grave, and when, in the early spring, the sun melted it away, her father took another wife.

This new wife brought two daughters with her, beautiful and fair to look upon, but dark and ugly in their hearts. Evil times were about to begin for the poor stepchild.

"Is this stupid creature to sit in the same room with *us*?" the stepsisters asked. "Those who eat must work for their supper. Let her be the kitchen maid."

They took away her pretty dresses and made her wear an old gray smock and wooden shoes.

"Just look at the proud princess now!" they laughed, and they banished her to the kitchen. There, she did all the heavy work, from morning to night. She had to rise up early in the morning, draw water, make the fires, cook, and wash. Besides that, the sisters did their utmost to torment her. They would toss dried peas and lentils among the ashes of the fire and order her to pick up every last one. In the evenings, when she was tired from her hard day's work, she had no bed to lie on but had to sleep on the hearth among the cinders. And because she always looked dusty and dirty, they called her Aschenputtel.

One day her father was leaving for the fair, and he asked his two stepdaughters what he should bring back for them.

"Fine clothes!" said the first.

"Pearls and jewels!" said the second.

"But what will you have, Aschenputtel?" he asked.

"The first twig, father, that strikes against your hat on the way home. That is what I should like you to bring me."

So he bought fine clothes, pearls, and jewels for the two stepdaughters, and on his way back, as he rode down a green lane, a hazel branch struck against his hat, and he broke it off and carried it home with him. He gave the stepdaughters what they had asked for, and to Aschenputtel he gave the hazel branch. She thanked him, then rushed to her mother's grave and planted the branch there, crying so much that her tears fell upon the ground and watered the branch so that it flourished and became a lovely tree. Aschenputtel went to sit under the tree three times each day, and wept, and prayed. A white bird would come to the tree, and if she uttered any wish, the bird brought her whatever she had wished for.

It came to pass that the king announced a dance and a festival that would last for three days, and to which all the beautiful young women of that country were invited, in order that the king's son might choose a bride from among them. When the two stepdaughters heard that they were invited, they were pleased and delighted, and they called at once for Aschenputtel.

"Comb our hair, brush our shoes, and make our buckles fast," they told her. "For we are going to the dance at the king's castle, and the prince will be choosing a bride."

When she heard this, Aschenputtel could not help crying, for she too would have liked to go to the dance, and she begged her stepmother to give her permission.

"You, Aschenputtel?" she laughed. "You in all your dust and dirt? You want to go to the festival? You that have no fine dress and no good shoes? You want to dance?"

But she wouldn't stop asking, so the stepmother said at last, "I have strewn a dishful of lentils in the ashes, and if you can pick them all up again in two hours, you may go with us."

Then the girl went to the back door that led into the garden and called out,

You gentle doves,
You turtledoves,
And all birds under heaven!
Come help me if you can.

Then two white doves came to the kitchen window, and after them some turtledoves, and at last a fluttering crowd of all the birds under heaven, and they alighted among the ashes. The doves nodded with their heads and began to peck, peck, peck, peck, and then all the others began to peck, peck, peck, peck and put all the grains into a dish. In scarcely an hour, the job was finished, and away they flew.

Then the girl brought the dish to her stepmother, thinking happily that now she would be able to go to the feast.

"No, Aschenputtel," the stepmother said. "You have no proper clothes, and you do not know how to dance, and everyone would laugh at you!"

But Aschenputtel wept again, so the woman said, "Very well. If you can pick two dishes of lentils out of the ashes in hour, you may go with us." She thought, of course, that this was not possible, and she tossed two dishes full of lentils among the ashes. Then Aschenputtel went through the back door into the garden and cried,

You gentle doves,
You turtledoves,
And all birds under heaven!
Come help me if you can.

Two white doves came to the kitchen window, and then some turtledoves, and at last a fluttering crowd of all the other birds under heaven. They alighted among the ashes, and the doves nodded with their heads and began to peck, peck, peck, peck, and then all the others began to peck, peck, peck, peck and put all the lentils back into the two dishes. And within half an hour their task was finished, and they flew away. Aschenputtel took the dishes to her stepmother, thinking happily that now she would be able to go with them to the dance. But the evil woman just said, "Even this is of no good to you. You cannot come with us, for you have no proper clothes, and cannot dance. You would put us to shame." Turning their backs on poor Aschenputtel, the three of them left without her.

Aschenputtel rushed to her mother's grave under the hazel tree and said,

Shake and shiver, little tree,
Let gold and silver fall on me.

Then the bird threw down a dress of gold and a pair of slippers embroidered with silk and silver. Quickly Aschenputtel put on the dress and rushed off to the dance. When she got there, even her own step-mother and sisters did not recognize her, and they thought she must be a princess, for she looked so beautiful in her golden dress. They gave no  thought at all to Aschenputtel, supposing that she was sitting at home and picking lentils out of the ashes.

The king's son came at once, and took her by the hand, and danced with her, and he would not dance with anyone else. And when any other man came to ask her to dance, he answered, "No, she is *my* partner."

Aschenputtel danced until evening came, then she wanted to go home, but the prince said he would accompany her, for he wanted to see where she lived. But Aschenputtel ran ahead of him and jumped up into the doves' house. The prince waited there until her father came and told him that a beautiful stranger had jumped into the doves' house.

"Could that be Aschenputtel?" the father thought to himself, and he called for axes and hatchets and had the doves' house cut down, but there was no one inside. And when they entered the kitchen, there sat Aschenputtel in her dirty clothes among the cinders, and a little oil lamp burnt dimly in the chimney. For Aschenputtel had been very quick, and had jumped out of the doves' house, run to the hazel bush, laid her beautiful dress upon the grave, and the bird had carried it away. Then she had put on her little gray smock again and had sat down in the kitchen among the cinders.

The next day, when the festival had begun anew, and the stepmother and stepsisters had departed, Aschenputtel went to the hazel bush and cried,

> Shake and shiver, little tree,
> Let gold and silver fall on me.

Then the bird cast down a dress still more splendid than the last, and when Anschenputtel appeared at the dance, everyone was astonished at her beauty. The prince had been waiting for her to come, and he took her hand and danced with her alone. And when anyone else came to ask her to dance, he said, "No, she is *my* partner."

And when the evening came she wanted to go home, and the prince followed her, for he wanted to know where she lived. But she broke away from him and ran into the garden at the back of the house, where there stood a large pear tree. She leapt up among the branches like a squirrel, and the prince did not know what had become of her. He waited until the father came, and then he told him that the strange maiden had again escaped from him and had climbed up into the pear tree.

"Could it be Aschenputtel?" the father thought to himself, and he called for an axe and felled the tree, but there was no one in it. And when they went into the kitchen, there sat Aschenputtel among the ashes, as usual, for she had climbed down the other side of the tree, and had taken back her beautiful clothes to the bird in the hazel bush, and had put on her old gray smock again.

On the third day, when the stepmother and stepsisters had left, Aschenputtel went again to her mother's grave and said to the hazel tree,

Shake and shiver, little tree,
Let gold and silver fall on me.

Then the bird cast down a dress, the like of which had never been seen for splendor and brilliance, and slippers of pure gold. And when Aschenputtel appeared in this dress at the dance, everyone was overcome with admiration for her. The prince danced with her alone, and if anyone else asked her to dance, he answered, "No, she is *my* partner."

And when it was evening, Aschenputtel wanted to go home, and the prince was about to go with her, when she ran past him so quickly that he could not follow her. But he had laid a trap for her and had caused all the palace steps to be smeared with sticky pitch, so that as she ran away, her left shoe remained stuck there. The prince ran and picked it up, and saw that it was made of gold and very small and slender. The next morning he went to his father and told him that he would marry only the young woman whose foot would fit the golden shoe.

When the prince came to their house, the two stepsisters rejoiced, for each was sure the slipper would fit her lovely foot. The eldest went to her room to try on the shoe, but she could not even get her big toe into it, for the shoe was too small.

Then her mother handed her a knife and said, "Cut the toe off, for once you are queen you will never have to walk again."

So the girl cut her toe off, squeezed her foot into the shoe, and, hiding her pain, she went down to the prince. Then he took her with him on the horse as his bride and rode off. They had to pass by the grave, and there sat the two doves on the hazel bush, and they sang out,

Turn around and look!
There is blood on her shoe.
The shoe is too small,
She's not the bride for you.

The prince looked at her shoe and saw the blood flowing. And he turned his horse round and took the false bride home again, saying she was not the right one, and that the other sister must try on the shoe. So that sister went into her bedroom, and got her toes into the shoe, but her heel was too large. Then her mother handed her the knife, saying, "Cut a piece off your heel. When you are queen you will never have to walk."

So the girl cut a piece off her heel and thrust her foot into the shoe and, concealing her pain, went down to the prince, who took her before him on his horse and rode off. When they passed by the hazel bush, the two doves sang out,

Turn around and look!
There is blood on her shoe.
The shoe is too small,
She's not the bride for you.

Then the prince looked at her foot and saw how the blood was flowing from the shoe and staining the white stocking. And he turned his horse round and brought the false bride home again. "This is not the right one," said he, "have you no other daughter?"

"No," said the man, "except that my dead wife left us a little homely cinder maid named Aschenputtel. But it isn't possible that she could be your bride." The king's son demanded to see her, but the stepmother said, "Oh, no! She is much too dirty. I could not let her be seen." But the king's son insisted, and so Aschenputtel had to appear.

First she washed her hands and face quite clean, and went in and curtseyed to the prince, who held out to her the golden shoe. Then she sat down on a stool, drew her foot out of the heavy wooden shoe, and slipped it into the golden one, which fitted it perfectly. And when she stood up, the prince looked in her face and recognized the beautiful stranger that had danced with him, and he cried, "This is the right bride!"

The stepmother and the two sisters grew pale with anger as the king's son put Aschenputtel before him on his horse and rode off. And as they passed the hazel bush, the two white doves cried,

Turn around and look!
No blood is on her shoe
The shoe is not too small,
She's the right bride for you.

The two doves flew down and perched on Aschenputtel's shoulders, one on the right, the other on the left, and there they stayed.

And when the wedding was held, the stepsisters came, hoping to win favor and to take part in the celebration. As the bridal procession approached the church, the elder sister walked on the right side and the younger on the left, and the doves pecked out an eye of each of them. And as the wedding procession returned from the church, the elder sister was on the left and the younger on the right, and the doves pecked out the other eye of each of them. And so they were condemned to go blind for the rest of their days because of their wickedness and falsehood.

Allerleirauh,
or the Many-furred Creature

Allerleirauh, from the German folktale collection of Jacob and Wilhelm Grimm is similar to the French tale, "Peu d'Anisso," in this collection. The heroines of this type of Cinderella tale are usually kings' or rich men's daughters. They receive priceless dresses from their fathers, but go forth into the world disguised as poor women, wearing the ugly skins of cats, bears, donkeys, or pelicans, or even garments made of grass or wood. The cloak of the Many-furred Creature is made from small pieces of fur, one bit from each of a thousand animals.

*T*here was once upon a time a king who had a wife with golden hair, and she was so beautiful that you couldn't find anyone like her in the world. It happened that she fell ill, and when she felt that she must soon die, she sent for the king and said, "If you want to marry after my death, make no one queen unless she is just as beautiful as I am and has just such golden hair as I have. Promise me this." After the king had promised her this, she closed her eyes and died.

For a long time the king was not to be comforted, and he did not even think of taking a second wife. At last his councillors said, "the king *must* marry again, so that we may have a queen." So messengers were sent far and wide to seek for a bride equal to the late queen in beauty. But there was no one in the wide world, and if there had been, she could not have had such golden hair. Then the messengers came home again, not having been able to find a queen.

Now the daughter, who was just as beautiful as her dead mother, had just such golden hair. One day when she had grown up, her father looked at her and saw that she was exactly like her mother. He said to his councillors, "I will marry my daughter, for she is exactly like her dead mother."

The councillors were angry and said, "God has forbidden a father to marry his daughter. No good can come from such evil, and ruin will fall upon the kingdom because of this."

The princess was still more shocked and quickly thought of a way to keep him from this plan. "Before I do your bidding," she told him, "I must have three dresses, one as golden as the sun, one as silver as the moon, and one as shining as the stars. Besides these, I want a cloak made of a thousand different kinds of skin. Every animal in your kingdom must give a bit of its skin to it." But she thought to herself, "This will be quite impossible." The king, however, was not to be turned from his purpose, and he commanded the most skilled maidens in his kingdom to weave the three dresses, one as golden as the sun, one as silver as the moon, and one as shining as the stars. And he gave orders to all his huntsmen to catch one of every kind of beast in the kingdom and to get a bit of its skin to make the cloak of a thousand pieces of fur. At last, when all was ready, the king commanded the cloak to be brought to him, and he spread it out before the princess and said, "Tomorrow shall be the wedding day."

When the princess saw that there was no more hope of changing her father's resolution, she determined to flee away. In the night, when everyone else was sleeping, she got up and took three things from her treasures—a gold ring, a little gold spinning-wheel, and a gold reel. She put the sun, moon, and star dresses in a nutshell, drew on the cloak of many skins, and made her face and hands dirty with soot. Then she commanded herself to God and went out and traveled the whole night till she came to a large forest. And as she was very much tired, she sat down inside a hollow tree and fell asleep.

The sun rose, and she still slept on and on, although it was nearly noon. Now, it happened that the king to whom this wood belonged was hunting in it. When his dogs came to the tree, they sniffed, and ran round and round it, barking. The king said to the huntsmen, "See what sort of a wild beast is in there." The huntsmen went in, and then came back and said, "In the hollow tree there lies a wonderful animal that we don't know, and we have never seen one like it. Its skin is made of a thousand pieces of fur, but it is lying down asleep." The king said, "See if you can catch it alive, and then fasten it to the cart, and we will take it with us."

When the huntsmen seized the maiden, she awoke and was frightened, and cried out to them, "I am a poor child, forsaken by father and mother. Take pity on me and let me go with you." Then they said to her, "Many-furred Creature, you can work in the kitchen. Come with us and sweep the ashes." So they put her in the cart and went back to the palace. There they showed her a tiny room under the stairs, where no daylight came, and said to her, "Many-furred Creature, you can live and sleep here." Then she was sent into the kitchen, where she carried wood and water, poked the fire, washed the vegetables, plucked fowls, swept up the ashes, and did all the dirty work.

It happened once when a great feast was being held in the palace that she said to the cook, "Can I go upstairs for a little bit and look on? I will stand outside the doors." The cook replied, "Yes, you can go up, but in half an hour you must be back here to sweep up the ashes." Then she took her little oil lamp, went into her little room, drew off her fur cloak, and washed off the soot from her face and hands, so that her beauty shone forth, and it was as if one sunbeam after another were coming out of a black cloud. Then she opened the nut and took out the dress as golden as the sun. And when she had done this, she went up to the feast, and everyone stepped out of her way, for nobody knew her, and they thought she must be a king's daughter. But the king came towards her and gave her his hand, and danced with her, thinking to himself, "My eyes have never beheld anyone so fair." When the dance was ended, she curtseyed to him, and when the king looked round she had disappeared, no one knew whither. The guards who were standing before the palace were called and questioned, but no one had seen her.

She had run to her little room and had quickly taken off her dress, made her face and hands dirty, put on the fur cloak, and was once more the Many-furred Creature. When she came into the kitchen and was setting about her work of sweeping the ashes together, the cook said to her, "Let that wait till tomorrow, just cook the king's soup for me. I want to have a little peep at the company upstairs. But be sure that you do not let a hair fall into it, otherwise you will get nothing to eat in the future!" So the cook went away, and the Many-furred Creature cooked the soup for the king. She made a bread soup as well as she possibly could, and when it was done, she fetched her gold ring from her little room and laid it in the tureen in which the soup was to be served up.

When the dance was ended, the king had his soup brought to him and ate it, and it was so good that he thought he had never tasted such soup in his life. But when he came to the bottom of the dish he saw a gold ring lying there, and he could not imagine how it got in. Then he commanded the cook to be brought before him. The cook was terrified when he heard the command and said to the Many-furred Creature, "You must have let a hair fall into the soup, and if you have, you deserve a good beating!"

When the cook came before the king, the king asked who had cooked the soup. The cook answered, "I cooked it." But the king said, "That' not true, for it was quite different and much better soup than you have ever cooked."

Then the cook said, "I must confess. I did not cook the soup. The Many-furred Creature did."

"Let her be brought before me," said the king.

When the Many-furred Creature came, the king asked who she was. "I am a poor child without father or mother," she replied. The king asked her what she did in the palace. "I am of no use except to have boots thrown at my head," she answered. Then he asked how she got the ring that was in the soup. "I know nothing at all about the ring," she said. So the king could find out nothing and was obliged to send her away.

After a time there was another feast, and the Many-furred Creature begged the cook to let her go once again and look on. The cook answered, "Yes, but come back again in half an hour, and cook the king the bread soup he likes so much."

So she ran away to her little room, washed herself quickly, took out of the nut the dress as silver as the moon, and put it on. Then she went upstairs looking just like a king's daughter, and the king came towards her, delighted to see her again, and they danced together. But when the dance was ended, she disappeared again so quickly that the king could not see which way she went. She ran to her little room and changed herself once more into the Many-furred Creature and went into the kitchen to cook the bread soup. When the cook was upstairs, she fetched the golden spinning wheel and put it in the dish so that the soup was poured over it. It was brought to the king, who ate it and liked it as much as the last time. He had the cook sent to him, and again the cook had to confess that the Many-furred Creature had cooked the soup. Then the Many-furred Creature came before the king, but she said that she knew nothing at all of the golden spinning wheel.

When the king had a feast for the third time, things did not turn out quite the same as at the other two. The cook said, "You must be a witch, Many-furred Creature, for you always put something in the soup so that it is much better and tastes nicer to the king than any that I cook." But because she begged hard, he let her go look at the dance again. Now she put on the dress as shining as the stars and stepped into the hall in it.

The king danced again with the beautiful maiden and thought she had never looked so beautiful. And while he was dancing, he put a gold ring on her finger without her seeing it, and he commanded that the dance should last longer than usual. When it was finished, he wanted to keep her hands in his, but she broke from him and sprang so quickly away among the people that she vanished from his sight. She ran as fast as she could to her little room under the stairs, but because she had stayed too long beyond the half hour, she could not stop to take off the beautiful dress but only threw the fur cloak over it, and in her haste she did not make herself quite dirty with the soot, one finger remaining clean. The Many-furred Creature now ran into the kitchen, cooked the king's bread soup, and when the cook had gone, she laid the gold reel in the dish. When the king found the reel at the bottom, he had the Many-furred Creature brought to him, and then he saw the lovely finger and the ring that he had put on her hand in the dance. Then he took her hand and held her tightly, and as she was trying to get away, she undid the fur cloak a little bit, and the star dress shone out. The king seized the cloak and tore it off her. Her golden hair came down, and she stood there in her full splendour and could not hide herself away anymore. And when the soot and ashes had been washed from her face, she looked more beautiful than anyone in the world. And the king said, "You are my dear bride, and we will never be separated from one another." So the wedding was celebrated, and they lived happily ever after.

Little One-eye, Little Two-eyes, and Little Three-eyes

Stories almost exactly like this one, featuring strange sisters with as many as nine eyes, have been collected from storytellers in many countries. Little Two-eyes is not a stepdaughter; she is treated badly by her real mother and sisters simply because she has the normal number of eyes and they do not! Little Two-eyes is sent out to tend an animal—a magic goat that will provide her with everything she needs to escape her cruel family.

This tale is from the German folktale collection of Jacob and Wilhelm Grimm.

*T*here was once upon a time a woman who had three daughters. The eldest was called Little One-eye, because she had only one eye in the middle of her forehead. The second was called Little Two-eyes, because she had two eyes like other people. And the youngest was Little Three-eyes, because she had three eyes, and her third eye was also in the middle of her forehead. But because Little Two-eyes did not look any different from other children, her sisters and mother would say to her, "You, with your two eyes, are no better than common folk. You don't belong to us." They pushed her about and gave her wretched old clothes to wear, and she got nothing to eat except what they left on their plates. They were as unkind to her as they could be.

It happened one day that Little Two-eyes had to go out into the fields to take care of the goat, but she was hungry because her sisters had given her so little to eat. So she sat down in the meadow and began to cry so hard that two little streams ran out of her eyes. When she looked up once, in her grief, a woman stood before her, who smiled and asked, "Little Two-eyes, why are you crying?"

Little Two-eyes answered, "Don't I have reason to cry? Because I have two eyes like other people, my sisters and my mother cannot stand me. They push me out of one corner into another and give me nothing to eat except what they leave. Today they gave me so little I am starving."

Then the wise woman said, "Little Two-eyes, dry your eyes. I will tell you something so you need never be hungry again. Only say to your goat,

> *Little goat, bleat,*
> *Little table, appear,*

and a table full of food will stand before you, and you can eat as much as you want. When you have had enough, you have only to say,

> *Little goat, bleat,*
> *Little table, away,*

and then it will vanish." Then the wise woman disappeared.

Little Two-eyes thought she should try at once and see if what the woman had told her was true, and she said,

> *Little goat, bleat,*
> *Little table, appear,*

and scarcely had she uttered the words, when a little table stood before her, covered with a white cloth, on which were arranged a plate, with a knife and a fork and a silver spoon, and the most beautiful dishes, which were smoking hot, as if they had just come out of the kitchen. Then Little Two-eyes said the shortest grace she knew and ate a good dinner. When she had eaten enough, she repeated what the wise woman had told her,

> *Little goat, bleat,*
> *Little table, away,*

and instantly the table and all that was on it disappeared. "This is a splendid way to keep house," said Little Two-eyes, and she was quite happy and contented.

In the evening, when she went home with her goat, she found a little earthenware dish with the food her sisters had left for her, but she didn't eat any of it. The next day, when she went out with her goat, she again left the few scraps on her plate untouched. At first her sisters did not notice, but finally they said, "Something is the matter with Little Two-eyes. She used to gobble up all that was given her, and now she just leaves her food. She must have found another way of getting something to eat." So Little One-eye was told to go out with Little Two-eyes when she drove the goat to pasture, to see whether anyone brought her food and drink.

Now when Little Two-eyes was leaving, Little One-eye came up to her and said, "I will go into the field with you and see if you take good care of the goat and if you drive him properly to get grass." But Little Two-eyes knew what Little One-eye had in her mind, and she drove the goat into the long grass and said, "Come, Little One-eye, we will sit down here and I will sing you something."

Little One-eye sat down. She wasn't used to walking so far on such a hot day, and when Little Two-eyes began singing,

Little One-eye, are you awake?
Little One-eye, are you asleep?

she shut her one eye and fell asleep. When Little Two-eyes saw Little One-eye was asleep, she said,

Little goat, bleat,
Little table, appear,

and sat down at her table and ate and drank as much as she wanted. Then she said again,

Little goat, bleat,
Little table, away,

and in the twinkling of an eye, all had vanished.

Little Two-eyes then woke Little One-eye and said, "Little One-eye, you meant to watch, but you went to sleep instead. In the meantime the goat could have run away. Come, we will go home."

So they went home. Little Two-eyes again left her little dish untouched. Little One-eye could not tell her mother why and said as an excuse, "Being outdoors made me sleepy."

The next day the mother said to Little Three-eyes, "This time you shall go with Little Two-eyes and watch what she does out in the fields and whether anyone brings her food and drink."

So Little Three-eyes went to Little Two-eyes and said, "I will go with you and see if you take good care of the goat and if you drive him properly to get grass."

But Little Two-eyes knew what Little Three-eyes had in her mind. She drove the goat out into the tall grass and said, "We will sit down here, Little Three-eyes, and I will sing you something." Little Three-eyes sat down. She was tired by the walk and the hot day. And Little Two-eyes sang the same little song again,

Little Three-eyes, are you awake?

but instead of singing as she should have,

Little Three-eyes, are you asleep?

she sang, without thinking,

> *Little Two-eyes, are you asleep?*

And she went on singing,

> *Little Three-eyes, are you awake?*
> *Little Two-eyes, are you asleep?*

The two eyes of Little Three-eyes fell asleep, but the third, which was not spoken to in the song, did *not* fall asleep. Of course, Little Three-eyes shut that eye also, to look as if she were asleep, but it was blinking and could see everything quite well.

When Little Two-eyes thought Little Three-eyes was sound asleep, she said her rhyme,

> *Little goat, bleat,*
> *Little table, appear,*

and ate and drank to her heart's content, and then made the table go away again by saying,

> *Little goat, bleat,*
> *Little table, away.*

But Little Three-eyes had seen everything. Then Little Two-eyes came to her, and woke her, and said, "Well, Little Three-eyes, have you been asleep? How well you watched me! Come, let's go home." When they reached home, Little Two-eyes did not eat again, and Little Three-eyes said to the mother, "I know now why that proud thing eats nothing. When she says to the goat in the field,

> *Little goat, bleat,*
> *Little table, appear,*

a table stands before her, spread with food much better than we have. When she has had enough, she says,

> *Little goat, bleat,*
> *Little table, away,*

and everything disappears again. I saw it all exactly. She made two of my eyes go to sleep with a little song, but the one in my forehead remained awake, luckily!"

Then the envious mother cried out, "Will you live better than we do, Little Two-eyes? You shall not have the chance to do so again!" She fetched a knife and killed the goat.

When Little Two-eyes saw this, she went out full of grief and sat down in the meadow weeping bitter tears. Then again the wise woman stood before her and said, "Little Two-eyes, why are you crying?"

"Have I not reason to cry?" she answered. "My mother has killed the goat that spread the table so beautifully before me when I sang the little song . . . Now I must go hungry again."

The wise woman said, "Little Two-eyes, I will give you a good piece of advice. Ask your sisters to give you the heart of the dead goat. Bury it in the earth before the house door. That will bring you good luck."

Then she disappeared, and Little Two-eyes went home and said to her sisters, "Dear sisters, do give me something of my goat. I ask nothing better than its heart."

They laughed and said, "You may have that if you want nothing more."

Little Two-eyes took the heart and in the evening, when all was quiet, buried it before the house door as the wise woman had told her. The next morning, when they all awoke, there stood a most wonderful tree, which had leaves of silver and fruit of gold growing on it—more lovely and gorgeous than anything ever seen. But only Little Two-eyes knew that it had sprung from the heart of the goat, for it was standing just where she had buried it in the ground.

Then the mother said to Little One-eye, "Climb up, my child, and break us off some fruit from the tree." Little One-eye climbed up, but just when she was going to take hold of one of the golden apples, the bough sprang out of her hands. And this happened every time, so that she could not break off a single apple, however hard she tried.

Then the mother said, "Little Three-eyes, you climb up. With your three eyes you can see better than Little One-eye." So Little One-eye slid down, and Little Three-eyes climbed up. But she was not any more successful. Try as she might, the golden apples bent themselves back. At last the mother grew impatient and climbed up herself, but she was even less successful than Little One-eye and Little Three-eyes in catching hold of the fruit and only grasped at the empty air.

Then Little Two-eyes said, "I will try just once, perhaps I shall succeed."

The sisters called out mockingly, "You with your two eyes will no doubt succeed!"

Little Two-eyes climbed up, and the golden apples did not jump away from her. They behaved properly so she could pluck them off, one after the other, and she brought a whole apronful down with her. The mother took them from her. But afterward, instead of behaving better toward poor Little Two-eyes, as they should have, they were jealous that only she could reach the fruit and were still more cruel.

It happened one day, when they were all standing together by the tree, that a young knight came riding along. "Be quick, Little Two-eyes," cried the two sisters. "Creep under this so you shall not disgrace us." They put poor Little Two-eyes under an empty barrel, and they pushed the golden apples that she had broken off under with her. When the knight, who was a very handsome young man, rode up, he wondered to see the marvelous tree of gold and silver and said to the two sisters,

"Whose beautiful tree is this? The one who will give me a twig of it shall have whatever she wants."

Then Little One-eye and Little Three-eyes answered that the tree belonged to them, and they would certainly break him off a twig. They gave themselves a great deal of trouble, but in vain. The twigs and fruit bent back every time from their hands.

Then the knight said, "It is very strange that the tree should belong to you, and yet you cannot take anything from it!"

But they insisted the tree was theirs. While they were saying this, Little Two-eyes rolled a couple of golden apples from under the barrel so they landed at the knight's feet. When the knight saw the apples, he was astonished and asked where they came from. Little One-eye and Little Three-eyes answered that they had another sister, but she could not be seen because she had only two eyes, like ordinary people.

But the knight demanded to see her and called out, "Little Two-eyes, come forth."

Then Little Two-eyes came out from under the barrel quite happily. The knight was astonished at her great beauty and said, "Little Two-eyes, I am sure you can break me off a twig from the tree."

"Yes," answered Little Two-eyes, "I can, for the tree is mine." So she climbed up and broke off a small branch with its silver leaves and golden fruit and gave it to the knight.

Then he said, "Little Two-eyes, what shall I give you for this?"

"Ah," answered Little Two-eyes, "I suffer hunger and thirst, want and sorrow, from early morning till late in the evening. If you would take me away with you, I should be happy!"

Then the knight lifted Little Two-eyes onto his horse and took her home to his father's castle. There he gave her beautiful clothes and food and drink, and because he loved her so much, he married her, and the wedding was celebrated with great joy.

When the handsome knight carried Little Two-eyes away with him, the two sisters envied her good luck at first. "But the wonderful tree is still with us after all," they said. "Although we cannot break any fruit from it, everyone will stop and look at it and will come to us and praise it. Who knows whether we may not reap a harvest from it?"

But the next morning the tree had flown and their hopes with it. When Little Two-eyes looked out of her window there it stood underneath, to her great delight. Little Two-eyes lived happily for a long time.

Once two poor women came to the castle begging. Little Two-eyes looked at them and recognized both her sisters, Little One-eye and Little Three-eyes, who had become so poor they had to ask for bread at her door. But Little Two-eyes welcomed them and was so good to them they both repented from their hearts of having been so unkind to their sister.

Cap o' Rushes

"Cap o' Rushes" is a folktale collected in the English countryside in the late 1800s, and it is told in the regional dialect of the storyteller. If you have trouble understanding the words, try reading them aloud to get the sense. Cap o' Rushes is the name of the heroine when she is disguised as a servant. She really wears a *cape*, not a cap, of rushes, or dried grasses. In this type of Cinderella tale, the heroine is driven out of the house by her father, who becomes angry when she tells him she loves him "as much as meat loves salt." At her wedding feast, Cap o' Rushes finds a way to let her father know exactly how nasty meat can taste without salt.

Well, there was once a very rich gentleman, and he had three daughters, and he thought he'd see how fond they were of him. So he says to the first, "How much do *you* love me, my dear?"

"Why," says she, "as I love my life."

"That's good," says he.

So he says to the second, "How much do *you* love me, my dear?"

"Why," says she, "better nor all the world."

"That's good," says he.

So he says to the third, "How much do *you* love me, my dear?"

"Why, I love you as fresh meat loves salt," says she.

Well, but he was angry. "You don't love me at all," says he, "and in my house you stay no more." So he drove her out there and then, and shut the door in her face.

Well, she went away on and on till she came to a fen, and there she gathered a lot of rushes and made them into a kind of a sort of a cloak with a hood, to cover her from head to foot, and to hide her fine clothes. And then she went on and on till she came to a great house.

"Do you want a maid?" says she.

"No, we don't," said they.

"I haven't nowhere to go," says she, "and I ask no wages, and do any sort of work."

"Well," said they, "if you like to wash the pots and scrape the saucepans you may stay," said they.

So she stayed there and washed the pots and scraped the saucepans and did all the dirty work. And because she gave no name they called her "Cap o' Rushes."

Well, one day there was to be a great dance a little way off, and the servants were allowed to go and look on at the grand people. Cap o' Rushes said she was too tired to go, so she stayed at home.

But when they were gone she offed with the cap o' rushes and cleaned herself, and went to the dance. And no one there was so finely dressed as she.

Well, who should be there but her master's son, and what should he do but fall in love with her the minute he set eyes on her. He wouldn't dance with anyone else.

But before the dance was done Cap o' Rushes slipped off, and away she went home. And when the other maids came back she was pretending to be asleep with her cap o' rushes on.

Well, next morning they said to her, "You did miss a sight, Cap o' Rushes!"

"What was that?" says she.

"Why, the beautifullest lady you ever did see, dressed right gay. The young master, he never took his eyes off her."

"Well, I should have liked to have seen her," says Cap o' Rushes.

"Well, there's to be another dance this evening, and perhaps she'll be there."

But, come the evening, Cap o' Rushes said she was too tired to go with them. Howsoever, when they were gone, she offed with her cap o' rushes and cleaned herself, and away she went to the dance.

The master's son had been reckoning on seeing her, and he danced with no one else, and never took his eyes off her. But, before the dance was over, she slipped off, and home she went, and when the maids came back she pretended to be asleep with her cap o' rushes on.

Next day they said to her again, "Well, Cap o' Rushes, you should ha' been there to see the lady. There she was again, and the young master he never took his eyes off her."

"Well, there," says she, "I should have like to have seen her."

"Well," says they, "there's a dance again this evening, and you must go with us, for she's sure to be there."

Well, come this evening, Cap o' Rushes said she was too tired to go, and do what they would she stayed at home. But when they were gone she offed with her cap o' rushes and cleaned herself, and away she went to the dance.

The master's son was rarely glad when he saw her. He danced with none but her and never took his eyes off her. When she wouldn't tell him her name, nor where she came from, he gave her a ring and told her if he didn't see her again he should die.

Well, before the dance was over, off she slipped, and home she went, and when the maids came home she was pretending to be asleep with her cap o' rushes on.

Well, next day they says to her, "There, Cap o' Rushes, you didn't come last night, and now you won't see the lady, for there's no more dances."

"Well I should have rarely liked to have seen her," says she.

The master's son he tried every way to find out where the lady was gone, but go where he might, and ask whom he might, he never heard anything about her. And he got worse and worse for the love of her till he had to keep his bed.

"Make some gruel for the young master," they said to the cook. "He's dying for the love of the lady." The cook she set about making it when Cap o' Rushes came in.

"What are you a-doing of?" says she.

"I'm going to make some gruel for the young master," says the cook, "for he's dying for love of the lady."

"Let me make it," says Cap o' Rushes.

Well, the cook wouldn't at first, but at last she said yes, and Cap o' Rushes made the gruel. And when she had made it, she slipped the ring into it on the sly before the cook took it upstairs.

The young man he drank it and then he saw the ring at the bottom.

"Send for the cook," says he.

So up she comes.

"Who made this gruel here?" says he.

"I did," says the cook, for she was frightened.

And he looked at her.

"No, you didn't," says he. "Say who did it, and you shan't be harmed."

"Well, then, 'twas Cap o' Rushes," says she.

"Send Cap o' Rushes here," says he.

So Cap o' Rushes came.

"Did you make my gruel?" says he.

"Yes, I did," says she.

"Where did you get this ring?" says he.

"From him that gave it to me," says she.

"Who are you, then?" says the young man.

"I'll show you," says she. And she offed with her cap o' rushes, and there she was in her beautiful clothes.

Well, the master's son he got well very soon, and they were to be married in a little time. It was to be a very grand wedding, and every one was asked far and near. And Cap o' Rushes' father was asked. But she never told anybody who she was.

But before the wedding she went to the cook, and says she,

"I want you to dress every dish without a mite o' salt."

"That'll be rare nasty," says the cook.

"That doesn't signify," says she.

"Very well," says the cook.

Well, the wedding day came, and they were married. And after they were married all the company sat down to the dinner. When they began to eat the meat, it was so tasteless they couldn't eat it. But Cap o' Rushes' father tried first one dish and then another, and then he burst out crying.

"What is the matter?" said the master's son to him.

"Oh!" says he, "I had a daughter. And I asked her how much she loved me. And she said 'As much as fresh meat loves salt.' And I turned her from my door, for I thought she didn't love me. And now I see she loved me best of all. And she may be dead for aught I know."

"No, father, here she is!" says Cap o' Rushes. And she goes up to him and puts her arms round him.

And so they were happy ever after.

Billy Beg and the Bull

Billy Beg is one of the few boy Cinderellas, and his adventures are very different from those of girls in Cinderella tales. The story was translated into English and written down by Seumas MacManus, who had heard the tale told in the Irish language when he was growing up. You will notice some unusual strings of words that are repeated many times throughout the story, for example, ". . . where you wouldn't have known day by night or night by day, over high hills, low hills, sheep-walks, and bullock-traces, the Cove of Cork, and old Tom Fox and his bugle horn." These are called *runs*. They are part sense and part nonsense, a unique feature of Irish storytelling.

The henwife, a worker of magic somewhat like a fairy godmother, is evil in this tale, while a henwife is a good helper in the next tale, "Fair, Brown and Trembling," which also comes from Ireland.

*O*nce on a time when pigs was swine, there was a king and a queen, and they had one son, Billy, and the queen gave Billy a bull that he was very fond of, and it was just as fond of him. After some time the queen died, and she put it as her last request on the king that he would never part Billy and the bull, and the king promised that, come what might, come what may, he would not. After the queen died the king married again, and the new queen didn't take to Billy Beg, and no more did she like the bull, seeing himself and Billy so thick. But she couldn't get the king on no account to part Billy and the bull, so she consulted with a henwife what they could do as regards separating Billy and the bull.

"What will you give me," says the henwife, "and I'll very soon part them?"

"Whatever you ask," says the queen.

"Well and good then," says the henwife, "you are to take to your bed, making pretend that you are bad with a complaint, and I'll do the rest of it."

And, well and good, to her bed she took, and none of the doctors could do anything for her, or make out what was her complaint. So the Queen asked for the hen-wife to be sent for. And sent for she was, and when she came in and examined the queen, she said there was one thing, and only one, could cure her. The king asked what was that, and the hen-wife said it was three mouthfuls of the blood of Billy Beg's bull. But the king wouldn't on no account hear of this, and the next day the queen was worse, and the third day she was worse still, and told the king she was dying, and he'd have her death on his head. So, sooner nor this, the king had to consent to Billy Beg's bull being killed. When Billy heard this he got very down in the heart entirely, and he went doitherin' about, and the bull saw him, and asked him what was wrong with him that he was so mournful, so Billy told the bull what was wrong with him, and the bull told him to never mind, but keep up his heart, the queen would never taste a drop of his blood. The next day then the bull was to be killed, and the queen got up and went out to have the delight of seeing his death. When the bull was led up to be killed, says he to Billy, "Jump up on my back till we see what kind of a horseman you are."

Up Billy jumped on his back, and with that the bull leapt nine mile high, nine mile deep and nine mile broad, and came down with Billy sticking between his horns. Hundreds were looking on dazed at the sight, and through them the bull rushed over the top of the queen, killing her dead, and away he galloped where you wouldn't know day by night or night by day, over high hills, low hills, sheep-walks, and bullock-traces, the Cove of Cork, and old Tom Fox with his bugle horn. When at last they stopped, "now then," says the bull to Billy, "you and I must undergo great scenery, Billy. Put your hand," says the bull, "in my left ear, and you'll get a napkin, that, when you spread it out, will be covered with eating and drinking of all sorts, fit for the king himself."

Billy did this, and then he spread out the napkin and ate and drank to his heart's content, and he rolled up the napkin and put it back in the bull's ear again.

"Then," says the bull, "now put your hand into my right ear and you'll find a bit of a stick. If you wind it over your head three times, it will be turned into a sword and give you the strength of a thousand men besides your own, and when you have no more need of it as a sword, it will change back into a stick again."

Billy did all this.

Then says the bull, "At twelve o'clock the morrow I'll have to meet and fight a great bull."

Billy then got up again on the bull's back, and the bull started off and away where you wouldn't know day by night or night by day, over high hills, low hills, sheep-walks and bullock-traces, the Cove of Cork, and old Tom Fox with his bugle horn. There he met the other bull, and both of them fought and the like of their fight was never seen before or since. They knocked the soft ground into hard, the hard into soft, the soft into spring wells, the spring wells into rocks, and the rocks into high hills. They fought long, and Billy Beg's bull killed the other and drank his blood. Then Billy took the napkin out of his ear again and spread it out and ate a hearty good dinner. Then says the bull to Billy, says he, "At twelve o'clock to-morrow, I'm to meet the bull's brother that I killed the day, and we'll have a hard fight."

Billy got on the bull's back again, and the bull started off and away where you wouldn't know day by night or night by day, over high hills, low hills, sheep-walks and bullock-traces, the Cove of Cork, and old Tom Fox with his bugle horn. There he met the bull's brother that he killed the day before, and they set to, and they fought, and the like of the fight was never seen before or since. They knocked the soft ground into hard, the hard into soft, the soft into spring wells, the spring wells into rocks, and the rocks into high hills. They fought long, and at last Billy's bull killed the other and drank his blood. And then Billy took out the napkin out of the bull's ear again and spread it out and ate another hearty dinner. Then says the bull to Billy, says he, "The morrow at twelve o'clock I'm to fight the brother to the two bulls I killed. He's a mighty great bull entirely, the strongest of them all. He's called the Black Bull of the Forest, and he'll be too able for me. When I'm dead," says the bull, "you, Billy, will take with you the napkin, and you'll never be hungry, and the stick, and you'll be able to overcome everything that comes in your way, and take out your knife and cut a strip of the hide off my back and another strip off my belly and make a belt of them, and as long as you wear them you cannot be killed."

Billy was very sorry to hear this, but he got up on the bull's back again, and they started off and away where you wouldn't know day by night or night by day, over high hills, low hills, sheep-walks and bullock-traces, the Cove of Cork, and old Tom Fox with his bugle horn.

And sure enough at twelve o'clock the next day they met the great Black Bull of the Forest, and both of the bulls to it, and commenced to fight, and the like of the fight was never seen before or since. They knocked the soft ground into hard ground, the hard ground into soft and the soft into spring wells, the spring wells into rocks, and the rocks into high hills. And they fought long. But at length the Black Bull of the Forest killed Billy Beg's bull and drank his blood. Billy Beg was so vexed at this that for two days he sat over the bull neither eating or drinking, but crying salt tears all the time. Then he got up, and he spread out the napkin and ate a hearty dinner for he was very hungry with his long fast. And after that he cut a strip of the hide off the bull's back, and another off the belly, and made a belt for himself, and taking it and the bit of stick and the napkin, he set out to push his fortune, and he traveled for three days and three nights till at last he come to a great gentleman's place. Billy asked the gentleman if he could give him employment, and the gentleman said he wanted just such a boy as him for herding cattle. Billy asked what cattle would he have to herd, and what wages would he get. The gentleman said he had three goats, three cows, three horses, and three asses that he fed in an orchard, but that no boy who went with them ever came back alive, for there were three giants, brothers, that came to milk the cows and the goats every day, and killed the boy that was herding. So if Billy liked to try, they wouldn't fix the wages till they'd see if he would come back alive.

"Agreed, then," said Billy.

So the next morning he got up and drove out the three goats, the three cows, the three horses, and the three asses to the orchard and commenced to feed them. About the middle of the day Billy heard three terrible roars that shook the apples off the bushes, shook the horns on the cows, and made the hair stand up on Billy's head, and in comes a frightful big giant with three heads, and begun to threaten Billy.

"You're too big," says the giant, "for one bite, and too small for two. What will I do with you?"

"I'll fight you," says Billy, says he stepping out to him and swinging the bit of stick three times over his head, when it changed into a sword and gave him the strength of a thousand men besides his own. The giant laughed at the size of him and says he, "Well, how will I kill you? Will it be by a swing by the back, a cut of the sword, or a square round of boxing?"

"A swing by the back," says Billy, "if you can."

So they both laid holds, and Billy lifted the giant clean off the ground, and fetching him down again, sunk him in the earth up to his arm-pits.

"Oh, have mercy," says the giant.

But Billy, taking his sword, killed the giant and cut out his tongues. It was evening by this time, so Billy drove home the three goats, three cows, three horses, and three asses, and all the vessels in the house wasn't able to hold all the milk the cows gave that night.

"Well," says the gentleman, "this beats me, for I never saw anyone coming back alive out of there before, nor the cows with a drop of milk. Did you see anything in the orchard?" says he.

"Nothing worse nor myself," says Billy. "What about my wages now."

"Well," says the gentleman, "you'll hardly come alive out of the orchard the morrow. So we'll wait till after that."

Next morning his master told Billy that something must have happened to one of the giants, for he used to hear the cries of three every night, but last night he only heard two crying.

"I don't know," says Billy, "anything about them."

That morning after he got his breakfast Billy drove the three goats, three cows, three horses, and three asses into the orchard again, and began to feed them. About twelve o'clock he heard three terrible roars that shook the apples off the bushes, the horns on the cows, and made the hair stand up on Billy's head, and in comes a frightful big giant with six heads, and he told Billy he had killed his brother yesterday, but he would make him pay for it the day.

"Ye're too big," says he, "for one bite, and too small for two, and what will I do with you?"

"I'll fight you," says Billy, swinging his stick three times over his head, and turning it into a sword, and giving him the strength of a thousand men besides his own. The giant laughed at him, and says he, "How will I kill you—with a swing by the back, a cut of the sword, or a square round of boxing?"

"With a swing by the back," says Billy, "if you can."

So the both of them laid holds, and Billy lifted the giant clean off the ground, and fetching him down again, sunk him in it up to the arm-pits.

"Oh, spare my life!" says the giant.

But Billy taking up his sword, killed him and cut out his tongues. It was evening by this time, and Billy drove home his three goats, three cows, three horses, and three asses, and what milk the cows gave that night overflowed all the vessels in the house, and, running out, turned a rusty mill that hadn't been turned before for thirty years. If the master was surprised seeing Billy coming back the night before, he was ten times more surprised now.

"Did you see anything in the orchard today?" says the gentleman.

"Nothing worse nor myself," says Billy. "What about my wages now," says Billy.

"Well, never mind about your wages," says the gentleman, "till the morrow, for I think you'll hardly come back alive again," says he. Well and good, Billy went to his bed, and the gentleman went to his bed, and when the gentleman rose in the morning says he to Billy, "I don't know what's wrong with two of the giants. I only heard one crying last night."

"I don't know," says Billy, "they must be sick or something."

Well, when Billy got his breakfast that day again, he set out to the orchard, driving before him the three goats, three cows, three horses, and three asses and sure enough about the middle of the day he hears three terrible roars again, and in comes another giant, this one with twelve heads on him, and if the other two were frightful, surely this one was ten times more so.

"You villain, you," says he to Billy. "You killed my two brothers, and I'll have my revenge on you now. Prepare till I kill you," says he. "You're too big for one bite, and too small for two. What will I do with you?"

"I'll fight you," says Billy, swinging the bit of stick three times over his head. The giant laughed heartily at the size of him, and says he, "What way do you prefer being killed? Is it with a swing by the back, a cut of the sword, or a square round of boxing?"

"A swing by the back," says Billy.

So both of them again laid holds, and my brave Billy lifts the giant clean off the ground, and fetching him down again, sunk him down to his arm-pits in it.

"Oh, have mercy. Spare my life," says the giant. But Billy took his sword, and killing him, cut out his tongues. That evening he drove home his three goats, three cows, three horses, and three asses, and the milk of the cows had to be turned into a valley where it made a lough three miles long, three miles broad, and three miles deep, and that lough has been filled with salmon and white trout ever since. The gentleman wondered now more than ever to see Billy back the third day alive.

"Did you see nothing in the orchard the day, Billy?" says he.

"No, nothing worse nor myself," says Billy.

"Well that beats me," says the gentleman.

"What about my wages now?" says Billy.

"Well, you're a good mindful boy, that I couldn't easy do without," says the gentleman, "and I'll give you any wages you ask for the future."

The next morning, says the gentleman to Billy, "I heard none of the giants crying last night, however it comes. I don't know what has happened to them."

"I don't know," says Billy. "They must be sick or something."

"Now, Billy," says the gentleman, "you must look after the cattle the day again, while I go to see the fight."

"What fight?" says Billy.

"Why," says the gentleman, "it's the king's daughter is going to be devoured by a fiery dragon, if the greatest fighter in the land, that they have been feeding specially for the last three months, isn't able to kill the dragon first. And if he's able to kill the dragon the king is to give him the daughter in marriage."

"That will be fine," says Billy. Billy drove out his three goats, three cows, three horses, and three asses to the orchard that day again. Billy never before witnessed the like of all the folks that passed by that day on their way to see the fight between the man and the fiery dragon. They went in coaches and carriages, on horses and jackasses, riding and walking, crawling and creeping.

"My tight little fellow," says a man that was passing to Billy, "why don't you come to see the great fight?"

"What would take the likes of me there?" says Billy.

But when Billy found them all gone, he saddled and bridled the best black horse his master had, and put on the best suit of clothes he could get in his master's house, and rode off to the fight after the rest. When Billy went there he saw the king's daughter with the whole court about her on a platform before the castle, and he thought he never saw anything half as beautiful, and the great warrior that was to fight the dragon was walking up and down on the lawn before her, with three men carrying his sword, and everyone in the whole country gathered there looking at him. But when the fiery dragon came up with twelve heads on him, and every mouth of him spitting fire, and let twelve roars out of him, the warrior ran away and hid himself up to the neck in a well of water, and for all they could do they couldn't get him to come and face the dragon.

Then the king's daughter asked if there was no one there to save her from the dragon and get her in marriage. But not one stirred. When Billy saw this, he tied the belt of the bull's hide round him, swung his stick over his head, and went in, and after a terrible fight entirely, killed the dragon. Every one then gathered about to find who the stranger was, but Billy jumped on his horse and darted away sooner than let them know. But just as he was getting away, the king's daughter pulled the shoe off his foot. When the dragon was killed, the warrior that had hid in the well of water came out, and cutting the heads off the dragon, he brought them to the king and said that it was he who killed the dragon, in disguise. And he claimed the king's daughter. But she tried the shoe on him and found it didn't fit him, so she said it wasn't him and that she would marry only the man the shoe fitted. When Billy got home he changed the clothes again, and had the horse in the stable, and the cattle all in before his master came. When the master came, he began telling Billy about the wonderful day they had entirely, and about the warrior hiding in the well of water, and about the grand stranger that came down out of the sky in a cloud on a black horse and killed the fiery dragon, and then vanished in a cloud again.

"And, now," says he, "Billy, wasn't that wonderful?"

"It was, indeed," says Billy, "very wonderful entirely."

After that it was given to over the country that all the people were to come to the king's castle on a certain day, and the king's daughter would try the shoe on them, and whoever it fitted she was to marry them. When the day arrived, Billy was in the orchard with the three goats, three cows, three horses, and three asses, as usual, and the like of all the crowds that passed that day going to the king's castle to get the shoe tried on, he never saw before. They went in coaches and carriages, on horses and jackasses, riding and walking, and crawling and creeping. They all asked Billy was he not going to the king's castle, but Billy said, "Arrah, what would be bringin' the likes of me there?"

At last when all the others had gone there passed an old man with a scarecrow suit of rags on him, and Billy stopped him and asked would he swap clothes with him.

"Just take care of yourself, now," says the old man, "and don't be playing off your jokes on my clothes, or maybe I'd make you feel the weight of this stick."

But Billy soon let him see it was in earnest he was, and both of them swapped suits. Then off to the castle started Billy, with the suit of rags on his back and an old stick in his hand, and when he came there he found all in great commotion trying on the shoe, and some of them cutting down their foot, trying to get it to fit. But it was all of no use, the shoe could be got to fit none of them at all, and the king's daughter was going to give up in despair when the wee ragged looking boy (which was Billy) elbowed his way through them and says he, "Let me try it on. Maybe it would fit me."

But the people when they saw him all began to laugh at the sight of him, and "Go along out of that, you example you," says they, shoving and pushing him back. But the king's daughter saw him and called on them by all manner of means to let him come up and try on the shoe. So Billy went up, and all the people looked on, breaking their hearts laughing at the conceit of it. But what would you have of it, but to the dumfounding of them all, the shoe fitted Billy as nice as if it was made on his foot for a last.

So the king's daughter claimed Billy as her husband. He then confessed that it was he that killed the fiery dragon, and when the king had him dressed up in a silk and satin suit, with plenty of gold and silver ornaments, everyone gave in that his like they never saw before. He was then married to the king's daughter, and the wedding lasted nine days, nine hours, nine minutes, nine half-minutes, and nine quarter-minutes, and they lived happy and well from that day to this. I got brogues of porridge and breeches of glass, a bit of pie for telling a lie, and then I came slithering home.

Fair, Brown, and Trembling

Trembling, the Cinderella of the tale, meets her prince not at a dance but at church, as do many of her cousins. Nor does she arrive safely in the happily-ever-after when she marries her prince. One of her evil sisters pushes her into the ocean and takes her place as the king's bride, while the unfortunate Trembling is swallowed by a whale. The cowboy who helps rescue her is not an American-style cowboy, but a young lad who tends a herd of cows.

Erin is another name for the land of Ireland, where this tale was collected from an Irish-speaking storyteller in 1887.

King Aedh Curucha lived in Tir Conal, and he had three daughters, whose names were Fair, Brown, and Trembling.

Fair and Brown had new dresses and went to church every Sunday. Trembling was kept at home to do the cooking and work. They would not let her go out of the house at all, for she was more beautiful than the other two, and they were in dread she might marry before themselves.

They carried on in this way for seven years. At the end of seven years, the son of the king of Omanya fell in love with the eldest sister.

One Sunday morning, after the other two had gone to church, the old henwife came into the kitchen to Trembling and said, "It's at church you ought to be this day, instead of working here at home."

"How could I go?" said Trembling. "I have no clothes good enough to wear at church, and if my sisters were to see me there, they'd kill me for going out of the house."

"I'll give you," said the henwife, "a finer dress than either of them has ever seen. And now tell me what dress will you have?"

"I'll have," said Trembling, "a dress as white as snow, and green shoes for my feet."

Then the henwife put on the cloak of darkness, clipped a piece from the old clothes the young woman had on, and asked for the whitest robes in the world and the most beautiful that could be found, and a pair of green shoes.

That moment she had the robe and the shoes, and she brought them to Trembling, who put them on. When Trembling was dressed and ready, the henwife said, "I have a honey-bird here to sit on your right shoulder, and a honey-finger to put on your left. At the door stands a milk-white mare, with a golden saddle for you to sit on, and a golden bridle to hold in your hand."

Trembling sat on the golden saddle, and when she was ready to start, the henwife said, "You must not go inside the door of the church, and the minute the people rise up at the end of Mass, do you make off and ride home as fast as the mare will carry you."

When Trembling came to the door of the church there was no one inside who could get a glimpse of her but was striving to know who she was, and when they saw her hurrying away at the end of Mass, they ran out to overtake her. But no use in their running. She was away before any man could come near her. From the minute she left the church till she got home, she overtook the wind before her and outstripped the wind behind.

She came down at the door, went in, and found the henwife had dinner ready. She put off the white robes and had on her old dress in a twinkling.

When the two sisters came home the henwife asked, "Have you any news today from the church?"

"We have great news," said they. "We saw a wonderful, grand lady at the church-door. The like of the robes she had we have never seen on a woman before. It's little that was thought of our dresses beside what she had on, and there wasn't a man at the church, from the king to the beggar, but was trying to look at her and know who she was."

The sisters would give no peace till they had two dresses like the robes of the strange lady, but honey-birds and honey-fingers were not to be found.

Next Sunday the two sisters went to church again and left the youngest at home to cook the dinner.

After they had gone, the henwife came in and asked, "Will you go to church today?"

"I would go," said Trembling, "if I could."

"What robe will you wear?" asked the henwife.

"The finest black satin that can be found, and red shoes for my feet."

"What color do you want the mare to be?"

"I want her to be so black and so glossy that I can see myself in her body."

The henwife put on the cloak of darkness and asked for the robes and the mare, and that moment she had them. When Trembling was dressed, the henwife put the honey-bird on her right shoulder and the honey-finger on her left. The saddle on the mare was silver and so was the bridle.

When Trembling sat in the saddle and was going away, the henwife ordered her strictly not to go inside the door of the church, but to rush away as soon as the people rose at the end of Mass and hurry home on the mare before any man could stop her.

That Sunday the people were more astonished than ever and gazed at her more than the first time; and all they were thinking of was to know who she was. But they had no chance, for the moment the people rose at the end of Mass she slipped from the church, was in the silver saddle, and home before a man could stop her or talk to her.

The henwife had the dinner ready. Trembling took off her satin robe and had on her old clothes before her sisters got home.

"What news have you today?" asked the henwife of the sisters when they came from the church.

"Oh, we saw the grand strange lady again! And it's little that any man could think of our dresses after looking at the robes of satin that she had on! And all at church, from high to low, had their mouths open, gazing at her, and no man was looking at us."

The two sisters gave neither rest nor peace till they got dresses as nearly like the strange lady's robes as they could find. Of course they were not so good, for the like of those robes could not be found in Erin.

When the third Sunday came, Fair and Brown went to church dressed in black satin. They left Trembling at home to work in the kitchen and told her to be sure and have dinner ready when they came back.

After they had gone and were out of sight, the henwife came to the kitchen and said, "Well, my dear, are you for church today?"

"I would go if I had a new dress to wear."

"I'll get you any dress you ask for. What dress would you like?" asked the henwife.

"A dress red as a rose from the waist down, and white as snow from the waist up; a cape of green on my shoulders, and a hat on my head with a red, a white, and a green feather in it; and shoes for my feet with the toes red, the middle white, and the backs and heels green."

The henwife put on the cloak of darkness, wished for all these things, and had them. When Trembling was dressed, the henwife put the honey-bird on her right shoulder and the honey-finger on her left, and placing the hat on her head, clipped a few hairs from one lock and a few from another with her scissors, and that moment the most beautiful golden hair was flowing down over the girl's shoulders. Then the henwife asked what kind of a mare she would ride. She said white, with blue and gold-colored diamond-shaped spots all over her body, on her back a saddle of gold, and on her head a golden bridle.

The mare stood there before the door, and a bird sitting between her ears, which began to sing as soon as Trembling was in the saddle and never stopped till she came home from the church.

The fame of the beautiful strange lady had gone out through the world, and all the princes and great men that were in it came to church that Sunday, each one hoping that it was himself would have her home with him after Mass.

The son of the king of Omanya forgot all about the eldest sister and remained outside the church, so as to catch the strange lady before she could hurry away.

The church was more crowded than ever before, and there were three times as many outside. There was such a throng before the church that Trembling could only come inside the gate.

As soon as the people were rising at the end of Mass, the lady slipped out through the gate and was in the golden saddle in an instant, sweeping away ahead of the wind. But if she was, the prince of Omanya was at her side, and, seizing her by the foot, he ran with the mare and never let go of the beautiful lady till the shoe was pulled from her foot, and he was left behind with it in his hand. She came home as fast as the mare could carry her and was thinking all the time that the henwife would kill her for losing the shoe.

Seeing her so vexed and so changed in the face, the old woman asked, "What's the trouble that's on you now?"

"Oh! I've lost one of the shoes off my feet," said Trembling.

"Don't mind that. Don't be vexed," said the henwife. "Maybe it's the best thing that ever happened to you."

Then Trembling gave up all the things she had to the henwife, put on her old clothes, and went to work in the kitchen. When the sisters came home, the henwife asked, "Have you any news from the church?"

"We have indeed," said they, "for we saw the grandest sight today. The strange lady came again, in grander array than before. On herself and on the horse she rode were the finest colors of the world, and between the ears of the horse was a bird which never stopped singing from the time she came till she went away. The lady herself is the most beautiful woman ever seen by man in Erin."

After Trembling had disappeared from the church, the son of the king of Omanya said to the other kings' sons, "I will have that lady for my own."

They all said, "You didn't win her just by taking the shoe off her foot, you'll have to win her by the point of the sword. You'll have to fight for her with us before you can call her your own."

"Well," said the son of Omanya, "when I find the lady that shoe will fit, I'll fight for her, never fear, before I leave her to any of you."

Then all the kings' sons were uneasy and anxious to know who was she that lost the shoe. And they began to travel all over Erin to find her. The prince of Omanya and all the others went in a great company together and made the round of Erin. They went everywhere—north, south, east, and west. They visited every place where a woman was to be found, and left not a house in the kingdom they did not search, to find the woman the shoe would fit, not caring whether she was rich or poor, of high or low degree.

The prince of Omanya always kept the shoe, and when the young women saw it, they had great hopes, for it was of proper size, neither large nor small, and it would beat any man to know of what material it was made. One thought it would fit her if she cut a little from her great toe, and another, with too short a foot, put something in the tip of her stocking. But no use—they only spoiled their feet and were curing them for months afterwards.

The two sisters, Fair and Brown, heard that the princes of the world were looking all over Erin for the woman that could wear the shoe, and every day they were talking of trying it on, and one day Trembling spoke up and said, "Maybe it's my foot that the shoe will fit."

"Oh, the breaking of the dog's foot on you! Why say so when you were at home every Sunday?"

They went on scolding their younger sister till the princes were near the place. The day they were to come, the sisters put Trembling in a closet and locked the door on her. When the company came to the house, the prince of Omanya gave the shoe to the sisters. But though they tried and tried, it would fit neither of them.

"Is there any other young woman in the house?" asked the prince.

"There is," said Trembling, speaking up from the closet. "I'm in here."

"Oh! We have her for nothing but to put out the ashes," said the sisters.

But the prince and the others wouldn't leave the house till they had seen her, so the two sisters had to open the door. When Trembling came out, the shoe was given to her, and it fitted exactly.

The prince of Omanya looked at her and said, "You are the woman the shoe fits, and you are the woman I took the shoe from."

Then Trembling spoke up, and said, "Stay here until I return."

Then she went to the henwife's house. The old woman put on the cloak of darkness, got everything for her she had the first Sunday at church, and put her on the white mare in the same fashion. Then Trembling rode along the highway to the front of the house. All who saw her the first time said, "This is the lady we saw at church."

Then she went away a second time, and a second time came back on the black mare in the second dress which the henwife gave her. All who saw her the second Sunday said, "That is the lady we saw at church."

A third time she asked for a short absence, and soon came back on the third mare and in the third dress. All who saw her the third time said, "That is the lady we saw in church." Every man was satisfied and knew that she was the woman.

Then all the princes and great men spoke up and said to the son of the king of Omanya, "You'll have to fight now for her before we let her go with you."

"I'm here before you, ready for combat," answered the prince.

Then the son of the king of Lochlin stepped forth. The struggle began, and a terrible struggle it was. They fought for nine hours, and then the son of the king of Lochlin stopped, gave up his claim, and left the field. Next day the son of the king of Spain fought six hours, and yielded his claim. On the third day the son of the king of Nyerfoi fought eight hours, and stopped. The fourth day the son of the king of Greece fought six hours, and stopped. On the fifth day no more strange princes wanted to fight, and all the sons of the king of Erin said they would not fight with a man of their own land, that the strangers had had their chance, and as no others came to claim the woman, she belonged of right to the son of the king of Omanya.

The marriage-day was fixed, and the invitations were sent out. The wedding lasted for a year and a day. When the wedding was over, the king's son brought home the bride, and when the time came a son was born. The young woman sent for her eldest sister, Fair, to be with her and care for her. One day, when Trembling was well, and when her husband was away hunting, the two sisters went out to walk. And when they came to the seaside, the eldest pushed the youngest in. A great whale came and swallowed her.

The eldest sister came home alone, and the husband asked, "Where is your sister?"

"She has gone home to her father in Ballyshannon. Now that I am well, I don't need her."

"Well," said the husband, looking at her, "I'm in dread it's my wife that has gone."

"Oh, no," said she, "It's my sister Fair that's gone."

Since the sisters were very much alike, the prince was in doubt. That night he put his sword between them, and said, "If you are my wife, this sword will get warm. If not, it will stay cold."

In the morning when he rose up, the sword was as cold as when he put it there.

It happened when the two sisters were walking by the seashore, that a little cow-boy was down by the water minding cattle and saw Fair push Trembling into the sea. And the next day, when the tide came in, he saw the whale swim up and throw her out on the sand. When she was on the sand she said to the cow-boy, "When you go home in the evening with the cows, tell the master that my sister Fair pushed me into the sea yester-day, that a whale swallowed me, and then threw me out. But he will come again and swallow me with the coming of the next tide. Then he'll go out with the tide, and come again with tomorrow's tide, and throw me again on the strand. The whale will cast me out three times. I'm under the enchantment of this whale and cannot leave the beach or escape myself. Unless my husband saves me before I'm swallowed the fourth time, I shall be lost. He must come and shoot the whale with a silver bullet when he turns on the broad of his back. Under the whale's fin is a reddish-brown spot. My husband must hit him in that spot, for it is the only place in which he can be killed."

When the cow-boy got home, the eldest sister gave him a drink of forgetfulness, and he did not tell.

Next day he went again to the sea. The whale came and cast Trembling on shore again. She asked the boy, "Did you tell the master what I told you to tell him?"

"I did not," said he. "I forgot."

"How did you forget?" asked she.

"The woman of the house gave me a drink that made me forget."

"Well, don't forget telling him this night, and if she gives you a drink, don't take it from her."

As soon as the cow-boy came home, the eldest sister offered him a drink. He refused to take it till he had delivered his message and told all to the master. The third day the prince went down with his gun and a silver bullet in it. He was not long down when the whale came and threw Trembling upon the beach as the two days before. She had no power to speak to her husband till he had killed the whale. Then the whale went out, turned over once on the broad of his back, and showed the spot for a moment only. That moment the prince fired. He had but the one chance, and a short one at that. But he took it and hit the spot, and the whale, mad with pain, made the sea all around red with blood and died.

That minute Trembling was able to speak and went home with her husband, who sent word to her father what the eldest sister had done. The father came and told him any death he chose to give her to give it. The prince told the father he would leave her life and death with himself. The father had her put out then on the sea in a barrel, with provisions in it for seven years.

In time Trembling had a second child, a daughter. The prince and she sent the cow-boy to school, and trained him up as one of their own children, and said, "If the little girl that is born to us now lives, no other man in the world will get her but him."

The cow-boy and the prince's daughter lived on till they were married. The mother said to her husband, "You could not have saved me from the whale but for the little cow-boy. On that account I don't grudge him my daughter."

The son of the king of Omanya and Trembling had fourteen children, and they lived happily till the two died of old age.

Hearth Cat

*L*ike many other Cinderellas, Hearth Cat has a magical helper who is a fish. When she tumbles into the well where the fish lives, Hearth Cat discovers a mysterious underworld kingdom where she obtains everything she needs to go to the ball being given at the palace. But unlike other animal helpers in Cinderella stories, this fish is not really a fish. Like the frog in another famous fairy tale, he is an enchanted prince.

The tale of "Hearth Cat" comes from Portugal.

*O*nce there was a widower who had three daughters. The two elder girls spent their time thinking of nothing but clothes and finery and of entertaining themselves. All day long they sat at the window, doing nothing. They left the youngest to take care of the house, and cook, and do all the work. Her sisters laughed at her and called her Hearth Cat.

One day the father caught a fish and brought it home alive. He gave it to the youngest daughter to cook for their supper, but she took a great liking to it on account of its pretty yellow color. She put it into a kettle of cool water, and she begged her father to let her keep it as a pet, and not kill it, until at length he agreed. She took the fish at once to her own room, and she watched happily as it swam about in the water. But when her sisters heard what had become of their dinner, they were furious and complained loudly that they had been deprived of eating an excellent fish.

That night, when Hearth Cat lay down to sleep, the fish began to call out to her, "Throw me into the well. Oh please, throw me into the well." The fish said this so sadly that at last Hearth Cat got up and took the fish out to the well and threw him in. The next day, she sat by the well, hoping to see the fish. She yearned to have a look at it once more, and as she leaned over the edge of the well, she heard a voice inside which said, "Oh maiden! Come into the well! Oh maiden! Come into the well!"

Hearth Cat ran away in fear, but on the following day, when her sisters were away, the maiden again sat by the edge of the well, and once more she heard the same voice calling to her. She leaned over further and further, until at last she fell into the well. She tumbled all the way to the bottom, where the fish appeared, swam around her in a circle, and led her to a palace made of gold and precious stones.

"Go into that chamber," he said, "and take the best and most elegant dress you find there, and put a pair of gold slippers on your feet. For your sisters have gone to a festival at the palace, and you must go there also."

After she had chosen a dress of gold and precious stones and put on the gold slippers, the fish showed her a splendid carriage and helped her inside.

"Take care to leave the festival before your sisters, and return at once to the well to take off your fine clothes. I promise you that a time is about to come when you will be as happy as you are now unhappy."

When Hearth Cat entered the palace, everyone fell back in admiration. They wondered aloud where such a beautiful creature could have come from, for no one had ever seen her before. She was careful to leave the palace at the very moment that the festival was over, but in her hurry to get out before her sisters, she lost one of her slippers. The king, who was following close behind her, picked it up and kept it. The next day, he issued a decree that he would marry the maiden who was the owner of that gold slipper.

When Hearth Cat reached home, she went quickly to the well, took off her rich garments, and put on her old ragged clothes again. The fish told her to return the next day, when her sisters were gone, for he wished to ask her something, and she promised that she would.

When her sisters returned home, Hearth Cat was once again busy in the kitchen. They talked on and on about the beautiful princess who had appeared at the feast, who had on such a beautiful dress all of gold and precious stones, and how this mysterious maiden had dropped one of her slippers in her hurry to leave. They told her that the king had sworn to marry the maiden to whom it belonged. Of course, they would to go to the palace and try it on—it might fit one of them, and surely they both deserved to be queen. Then, they might even buy Hearth Cat a new dress!

The moment the sisters left for the palace the next day, Hearth Cat went to the well to see the fish, who asked her at once, "Maiden, will you marry me?"

"How can I possibly marry a fish!" she exclaimed.

But he pleaded with her so long and looked at her so pitifully, that at last she agreed. And at once the fish was transformed into a handsome young man.

"Now you must know that I am a prince who was under an enchantment," he told her. "I am the son of the king of this land. I know that my father has ordered all the young women of the kingdom to come to the palace and try on the golden slipper that you dropped as you left the festival. Go there, and when the king tells you that you must marry him, tell him that you are already promised to the prince, his son, whom you have released from his enchantment."

Hearth Cat left the well and met her sisters who were returning from the palace, looking very downcast and disappointed because the slipper had not fit them. The maiden hinted that she, also, was thinking of going to the palace, just in case the slipper fit her.

"You should be ashamed of yourself, Hearth Cat!" said the one sister. "Go and show your dainty kitchen-maid's foot if you want," said the other. "Everyone will laugh at you."

When Hearth Cat arrived at the palace, the guards, seeing her so shabbily dressed, would not let her enter. But the king saw her from the window and ordered her to come in and try the slipper. It fitted her perfectly, of course. Then he asked her to marry him and be the queen. Very respectfully she told him that it could not be, for she was already promised to his majesty's son the prince, who had been spellbound long ago. The king could scarcely contain his delight to think that he would soon see his son again and sent a retinue of all the nobles of the realm to bring his son to the palace.

The wedding of the prince and Hearth Cat was celebrated with much feasting and rejoicing, while the two sisters remained at home, filled with jealousy and bitterness.

Katie Woodencloak

This tale was collected in Norway in the nineteenth century. Adventuresome Katie rides away from her evil stepmother on the back of a magic bull who is her friend and protector. Although the bull warns Katie not to pick any leaf or fruit in the magic forests of bronze, silver, and gold, the girl just can't help but disobey. When the heroes or heroines of a fairy tale are warned *not* to do something, they almost always do it. Notice that in this tale Katie does not just lose her slipper. The clever prince sets a trap to catch it.

*O*nce on a time there was a king who had become a widower. By his queen he had one daughter, who was so clever and lovely, there wasn't a cleverer or lovelier princess in all the world. So the king went on a long time sorrowing for the queen, whom he had loved so much, but at last he got weary of living alone and married another queen who was a widow and had, too, an only daughter. But this daughter was just as bad and ugly as the other was kind, clever, and lovely. The stepmother and her daughter were jealous of the princess, but so long as the king was at home they dared not do her any harm, for he was so fond of her.

Well, after a time, he fell into war with another king and went out to battle with his host, and then the stepmother thought she might do as she pleased. And so she both starved and beat the princess and sent her out to herd the cattle in the woods and on the fells. As for food, she got little or none, and she grew thin and wan and was always sobbing and sorrowful. Now, in the herd there was a great dun bull, who always kept himself neat and sleek, and often he came up to the princess and let her pat him. So one day when she sat there, sad and sobbing, he came up to her and asked her outright why she was always in such grief. She answered nothing, but went on weeping.

"Ah!" said the bull, "I know all about it quite well. You weep because the queen is bad to you, and because she is ready to starve you to death. But you've no need to fret about food, for in my left ear lies a cloth. Take it and spread it out, and you will have as many fine dishes as you please."

So she did that, took the cloth and spread it out on the grass, and lo! it served up the nicest dishes one could wish to have. There was wine too, and sweet cake. Well, she soon grew so plump and rosy that the queen and her scrawny chip of a daughter turned blue with spite. The Queen couldn't at all make out how her stepdaughter got to look so well on such little food, so she told one of her maids to follow her into the wood. So the maid went after her and watched in the wood, and then she saw how the stepdaughter took the cloth out of the bull's ear, and spread it out, and how it served up the nicest dishes, which the stepdaughter ate and made good cheer over. All this the maid told the queen when she went home.

And now the king came home from war and had won the fight against the other king with whom he went out to battle. So there was great joy throughout the palace, and no one was gladder than the king's daughter. But the queen shammed sick, and took to her bed, and paid the doctor a great fee to get him to say she could never be well again unless she had some of the dun bull's flesh to eat. Both the king's daughter and the folk in the palace asked the doctor if nothing else would help her and prayed hard for the bull, for everyone was fond of him, and they all said there wasn't that bull's match in all the land. But no, he must and should be slaughtered, nothing else would do. When the king's daughter heard that, she got very sorrowful and went down into the byre to the bull. There, too, he stood and hung down his head and looked so downcast that she began to weep over him.

"What are you weeping for?" asked the bull.

So she told him how the king had come home again, and how the queen had shammed sick and got the doctor to say she could never be well and sound again unless she got some of the dun bull's flesh to eat, and so now he was to be slaughtered.

"If they get me killed first," said the bull, "they'll soon take your life, too. Now, if you're of my mind, we'll just start off, and go away tonight."

Well, the princess thought it bad, you may be sure, to go and leave her father, but she thought it still worse to be in the house with the queen, and so she gave her word to the bull to come to him.

At night, when all had gone to bed, the princess stole down to the byre to the bull, and so he took her on his back and set off from the homestead as fast as ever he could. And when the folk got up at cockcrow next morning to slaughter the bull, why, he was gone. And when the king got up and asked for his daughter, she was gone too. He sent out messengers on all sides to hunt for them and gave them out in all the parish churches. But there was no one who had caught a glimpse of them. Meanwhile, the bull went through many lands with the king's daughter on his back, and so one day they came to a great copper wood, where both the trees, and branches, and leaves, and flowers, and everything, were nothing but copper.

But before they went into the wood, the bull said to the king's daughter,

"Now, when we get into this wood, mind you take care not to touch even a leaf of it, else it's all over both with me and you, for here dwells a troll with three heads who owns this wood."

No, bless her, she'd be sure to take care not to touch anything. Well, she was very careful, and leant this way and that to miss the boughs, and put them gently aside with her hands. But it was such a thick wood, 'twas scarce possible to get through, and so, with all her pains, somehow or other she tore off a leaf, which she held in her hand.

"AU! AU! What have you done now?" said the bull. "There's nothing for it now but to fight for life and death. But mind you, keep the leaf safe."

Soon after they got to the end of the wood, and a troll with three heads came running up.

"Who is this that touches my wood?" said the troll.

"It's just as much mine as yours," said the bull.

"Ah!" roared the troll, "We'll try a fall about that."

"As you choose," said the bull.

So they rushed at one another, and fought, and the bull he butted and gored and kicked with all high might and main. But the troll gave him as good as he brought, and it lasted the whole day before the bull got the mastery. And then he was so full of wounds, and so worn out, he could scarce lift a leg. Then they were forced to stay there a day to rest, and then the bull bade the king's daughter to take the horn of ointment which hung at the troll's belt and rub him with it. Then he came to himself again, and the day after they trudged on again. So they traveled many, many days, until, after a long, long time, they came to a silver wood, where both the trees, and branches, and leaves, and flowers, and everything, were silvern.

Before the bull went into the wood, he said to the king's daughter,

"Now, when we get into this wood, for heaven's sake mind you take good care. You mustn't touch anything, and not pluck off so much as one leaf, else it is all over both with me and you. For here dwells a troll with six heads who owns it, and him I don't think I should be able to master."

"No," said the king's daughter. "I'll take good care and not touch anything you don't wish me to touch."

But when they got into the wood, it was so close and thick, they could scarce get along. She was as careful as careful could be, and leant to this side and that to miss the boughs, and put them on one side with her hands, but every minute the branches struck her across the eyes, and in spite of all her pains, it so happened she tore off a leaf.

"AU! AU! What have you done now?" said the bull. "There's nothing for it now but to fight for life and death, for this troll has six heads and is twice as strong as the other, but mind you keep the leaf safe, and don't lose it."

Just as he said that, up came the troll.

"Who is this," he said, "that touches my wood?"

"It's as much mine as yours," said the bull.

"That we'll try a fall about," roared the troll.

"As you choose," said the bull, and he rushed at the troll, and gored out his eyes, and drove his horns right through his body, so that the entrails gushed out. But the troll was almost a match for him, and it lasted three whole days before the bull got the life gored out of the troll. But then he, too, was so weak and wretched, it was as much as he could do to stir a limb, and so full of wounds that the blood streamed from him. So he said to the king's daughter she must take the horn of ointment that hung at the troll's belt and rub him with it. Then she did that, and he came to himself. But they were forced to stay there a week to rest before the bull had strength enough to go on.

At last they set off again, but the bull was still poorly, and they went rather slow at first. So to spare time, the king's daughter said as she was young and light of foot, she could very well walk, but she couldn't get leave to do that. No, she must seat herself on his back again. So on they traveled through many lands a long time, and the king's daughter did not know in the least whither they went. But after a long, long time they came to a gold wood. It was so grand—the gold dropped from every twig, and all the trees, and boughs, and flowers, and leaves, were of pure gold. Here, too, the same thing happened as had happened in the silver wood and the copper wood. The bull told the king's daughter she mustn't touch it for anything, for there was a troll with nine heads who owned it, and he was much bigger and stouter than both the others put together, and he didn't think he could get the better of him. No, she'd be sure to take heed and not touch it.

But when they got into the wood, it was far thicker and closer than the silver wood, and the deeper they went into it, the worse it got. The wood went on getting thicker and thicker, and closer and closer, and at last she thought there was no way at all to get through it. She was in such an awful fright of plucking off anything, that she sat, and twisted and turned herself this way and that, and hither and thither, to keep clear of the boughs, and she put them on one side with her hands. But every moment the branches struck her across the eyes, so that she couldn't see what she was clutching at. Before she knew how it came about, she had a gold apple in her hand. Then she was so bitterly sorry she burst into tears and wanted to throw it away. But the bull said she must keep it safe and watch it well.

Just then up came the troll with the nine heads, and he was so ugly, the king's daughter scarcely dared to look at him.

"Who is this that touches my wood?" he roared.

"It's just as much mine as yours," said the bull.

"That we'll try a fall about," roared the troll again.

"Just as you choose," said the bull. And so they rushed at one another and fought, and it was such a dreadful sight the king's daughter was ready to swoon away. The bull gored out the troll's eyes and drove his horns through and through his body, till the entrails came tumbling out. But the troll fought bravely, and when the bull got one head gored to death, the rest breathed life into it again, and so it lasted a whole week before the bull was able to get the life out of them all. But then he was utterly worn out and wretched. He couldn't stir a foot, and his body was all one wound. He couldn't so much as ask the king's daughter to take the horn of ointment which hung at the troll's belt and rub it over him. But she did it all the same, and then he came to himself by little and little. But they had to lie there and rest three weeks before he was fit to go on again.

Then they set off at a snail's pace, for the bull said they had still a little farther to go, and so they crossed over many high hills and thick woods. So after a while they got upon the fells.

"Do you see anything?" asked the bull.

"No, I see nothing but the sky and the wild fell," said the king's daughter.

So when they clomb higher up, the fell got smoother, and they could see farther off.

"Do you see anything now?" asked the bull.

"Yes, I see a little castle far, far away," said the princess.

"That's not so little though," said the bull.

After a long, long time, they came to a great cairn, where there was a spur of the fell that stood sheer across the way.

"Do you see anything now?" asked the bull.

"Yes, now I see the castle close by," said the king's daughter, "and now it is much, much bigger."

"Thither you're to go," said the bull. "Right underneath the castle is a pigsty, where you are to dwell. When you come thither, you'll find a wooden cloak, all made of strips of lath; that you must put on, and go up to the castle and say your name is 'Katie Woodencloak,' and ask for a place. But before you go, you must take a knife and cut my head off, and then you must flay me, and roll up the hide, and lay it under the wall of rock yonder, and under the hide you must lay the copper leaf, and the silvern leaf, and the golden apple. Yonder, up against the rock, stands a stick. When you want anything, you've only got to knock on the wall of rock with that stick."

At first the princess wouldn't do anything of the kind. But when the bull said it was the only thanks he would have for what he had done for her, she couldn't help herself.

So however much it grieved her heart, she hacked and cut away with her knife at the big beast till she got both his head and his hide off, and then she laid the hide up under the wall of rock, and put the copper leaf, and the silvern leaf, and the golden apple inside it.

So when she had done that, she went over to the pigsty, but all the while she went she sobbed and wept. There she put on the wooden cloak, and so went up to the palace. When she came into the kitchen she begged for a place and told them her name was Katie Woodencloak. Yes, the cook said she might have a place. She might have leave to be there in the scullery, and wash up, for the lassie who did that work before had just gone away.

The following Sunday, there were to be guests at the palace, so Katie asked if she might have leave to carry up water for the prince's bath. The others laughed at her.

"What would you do there? Do you think the prince will care to look at you, you who are such a fright?"

But she wouldn't give it up, and kept on begging and praying, and at last she got leave. So when she went up the stairs, her wooden cloak made such a clatter, the prince came out and asked, "Pray, who are you?"

"Oh, I was just going to bring up water for your royal bath," said Katie.

"Do you think," said the prince, "that I would have anything to do with the water you bring?" And with that, he threw the water all over her.

So she had to put up with that, but then she asked leave to go to church. Well, she got that leave, too, for the church lay close by. But first of all she went to the rock and knocked on its face with the stick which stood there just as the bull had said. And straightaway out came a man, who asked what she wanted.

The princess said she had no clothes to go to church in. So he brought out a gown as bright as the copper wood, and a fine horse and saddle besides. When she got to the church, she was so lovely and grand that everyone wondered who she could be, and scarce one of them listened to the priest, for they all looked at her. As for the prince, he fell so deep in love with her, he didn't take his eyes off her for a single moment.

As she went out of church, the prince ran after her and held the church door open for her, and so he got hold of one of her gloves which was caught in the door. When she went away and mounted her horse, the prince went up to her again and asked whence she came.

"Oh, I'm from Bath Land," said Katie. And while the prince took out the glove to give it to her, she said,

Bright before and dark behind,
Clouds come rolling on the wind.
That this prince may never see
Where my good steed goes with me.

The prince had never seen the like of that glove and went about far and wide asking, but no one could tell him where Bath Land lay.

Next Sunday, someone had to go up to the prince with a towel.

"Oh, may I have leave to go up with it?" said Katie.

"What's the good of your going?" said the others. "You saw how it fared with you last time."

But Katie wouldn't give in; she kept on begging and praying, till she got leave. Then she ran up the stairs so that her wooden cloak made a great clatter. Out came the prince, and when he saw it was Katie, he tore the towel out of her hand and threw it into her face.

"Pack yourself off, you ugly troll," he cried. "Do you think I'd have a towel which you have touched with your smutty fingers?"

After that the prince set off to church, and Katie begged for leave to go too. They all asked what business she had at church—she who had nothing to put on but that wooden cloak, which was so black and ugly. But at last she got leave to go.

Now, she went again to the rock and knocked, and so out came the man and gave her a gown far finer than the first one. It was all covered with silver, and it shone like the silver wood, and she got besides a noble steed with a saddle cloth embroidered with silver, and a silver bit.

So when the king's daughter got to the church, the folk were still standing about in the churchyard. And all of them wondered who she could be. The prince was soon on the spot and came and wished to hold her horse for her while she got off. But she jumped down and said there was no need. So they all went into church, but there was scarce a soul that listened to what the priest said, for they looked at her a deal too much. And the prince fell still deeper in love than the first time.

When the sermon was over, and Katie left the church and was going to mount her horse, up came the prince again and asked where she came from.

"Oh, I'm from Towel Land," said the king's daughter, and as she said that, she dropped her riding whip, and when the prince stooped to pick it up, she said,

Bright before and dark behind,
Clouds come rolling on the wind.
That this prince may never see
Where my good steed goes with me.

So away she was again, and the prince couldn't tell what had become of her. He went about far and wide, asking after Towel Land, whence she said she came. But there was no one who could tell him where it lay.

Next Sunday someone had to go up to the prince with a comb. Katie begged for leave to go up with it, but the others put her in mind how she had fared the last time and scolded her for wishing to go before the prince—such an ugly fright she was in her wooden cloak. But she wouldn't leave off asking till they let her go up to the prince with his comb. So, when she came clattering up the stairs again, out came the prince, and took the comb, and threw it at her, and bade her be off as fast as she could. After that the prince went to church, and Katie begged for leave to go too.

So the same thing happened now as had happened twice before. She went to the rock and knocked with the stick, and then the man came out and gave her a gown which was far grander than either of the others. It was almost all pure gold and studded with diamonds. And she got besides a noble steed with a gold embroidered saddle and a golden bit.

Now when the king's daughter got to the church, there stood the priest and all the people in the churchyard waiting for her. Up came the prince running, and wanted to hold her horse, but she jumped off and said, "No, thank you."

So everyone hastened into church, and the priest got into the pulpit, but no one listened to a word he said, for they all looked too much at the king's daughter and wondered whence she came. The prince was far deeper in love than ever, and he sat and stared at her.

When the sermon was over, and the king's daughter was to go out of the church, the prince had already spread sticky pitch across the threshhold, so that she would have to let him carry her across it. But she didn't care a bit—she just put her foot right down into the midst of the pitch and jumped across it. But one of her golden shoes stuck fast in it. On she ran and jumped on her horse. The prince came running out of the church and asked from whence she came.

"I'm from Comb Land," said Katie. But when the prince tried to give her the little golden shoe, she said,

> *Bright before and dark behind,*
> *Clouds come rolling on the wind.*
> *That this prince may never see*
> *Where my good steed goes with me.*

So the prince couldn't tell still what had become of her, and he went about a weary time all over the world asking for Comb Land. And when no one could tell him, he ordered that it be announced far and wide that he would wed the woman whose foot could fit the golden shoe.

Many came of all sorts from all sides, fair and ugly alike. But there was none who had so small a foot as to be able to get on the gold shoe. And who should come but Katie's wicked stepmother and her daughter, too, and the golden shoe fitted her!

But she was so loathly, the prince hated to keep his word. Still, they got ready for the wedding feast, and the stepsister was dressed up and decked out as a bride. But as they rode to church, a little bird sat upon a tree branch and sang,

> *A bit off her heel*
> *And a bit off her toe!*
> *Katie Woodencloak's tiny shoe*
> *Is full of blood—that's all I know.*

Sure enough, when they looked to it, the bird told the truth, for blood gushed out of the shoe.

"Where is Katie Woodencloak?" asked the prince.

Katie came trampling upstairs, her wooden cloak clattering, and the other maids laughed and made fun of her.

Katie took up the shoe, and put her foot into it, and threw off her wooden cloak. There she stood in her gold gown, and it shone so that the sunbeams glistened from her. And lo! On her other foot she had the matching golden shoe.

The prince ran up to her and threw his arms round her and gave her a kiss. And when he heard she was a king's daughter, he got gladder still, and then came the wedding feast, and so,

> *Snip, snip, snover,*
> *This story's over.*

The Wonderful Birch

This exciting tale was told in Finland and was first written down in the nineteenth century. The heroine's evil stepmother is no mere human being, but a dangerous, cannibalistic, shape-shifting troll who turns the girl's real mother into a sheep. The stepsister is also a troll, of course, but a funny one who can't get used to human table manners. When she is given meat, she takes it under the table and chews on it like a dog!

*O*nce upon a time there lived a man and a woman who had an only daughter. It happened that one of their sheep went astray, and they set out to look for it, and searched and searched, each in a different part of the wood. Then the good woman met an troll, who recited a magic charm,

Spit into my knife-sheath,
Pass between my legs,
Turn into a black sheep.

Then the troll took on the woman's face and form. "I've found the sheep," she called out to the good man. The man believed the troll was his wife—he did not know that his wife was the sheep. Home they went, and when they got there the woman said, "Look here, old man, we must kill this sheep lest it run away to the woods again."

The man, who was a peaceable, quiet fellow, made no objection, but simply said, "Good, let us do so."

His daughter, however, overheard their talk and ran to the sheepfold. "Oh, dear little mother, they are going to slaughter you."

"Well, then, if they do," replied the black sheep, "do not eat the meat or broth, but only gather all my bones and bury them by the edge of the field."

Shortly after this they took the black sheep from the flock and slaughtered it. The troll made soup of it and set it before the daughter, but the girl remembered her mother's warning. She did not touch the soup, but she carried the bones to the edge of the field and buried them. And from the bones there sprang up a beautiful tree.

In the meanwhile, a daughter was born to the ogress, and the woman took a furious dislike to the man's daughter and began to torment her in every way.

It happened that a great festival was to be held at the palace, to which the king invited all the people thereabouts, even the most poor and wretched.

And so in the good man's house, preparations were made to go to the palace. The troll said, "Go along first, old man, with our younger daughter. I will give the elder girl some work to do, so that she won't be bored while we are away."

When the two of them had gone, the troll threw a bowl of barley grains among the cinders and said, "If you have not picked every grain of barley out of the ashes, and put it back into the bowl before nightfall, I shall eat you up!"

Then she hastened after the others, and the poor girl stayed at home and wept. She tried, to be sure, to pick up the grains of barley, but she soon saw how useless her labor was. And so she went to her mother's grave, and she cried because her mother could no longer help her. In the midst of her grief, she suddenly heard her mother's voice.

"Why do you weep, little daughter?"

"The troll has scattered barley on the hearth and ordered me to pick them out of the ashes," said the girl. "That is why I weep, dear mother."

"Do not weep," said her mother. "Break off a branch from the birch tree, strike the hearth with it crosswise, and all will be put right."

The girl did so. She struck the hearth with the branch, and the barley flew into the bowl, and the hearth was clean. Then she went back to the tree and laid the branch upon the grave. Then her mother's voice bade her to bathe on one side of the tree, dry herself on the other, then put on the clothes she found within the tree trunk.

After the girl had done all this, she became so lovely that no one on earth could rival her. Splendid clothing and jewels were given to her, and a horse with hair partly of gold, partly of silver, and partly of something more precious still. The girl sprang into the saddle and rode as swift as an arrow to the palace. As she turned into the courtyard of the castle, the king's son came out to meet her, tied her steed to a pillar, and led her in. He never left her side as they passed through the castle rooms. And all the people gazed at her, and wondered who the lovely maiden was, and from what castle she came. But no one knew anything about her.

At the banquet the prince invited her to sit next to him in the place of honor. Meanwhile, the troll's daughter had taken a piece of meat, crawled under the table, and was noisily gnawing the bones. The prince heard the sound, and, thinking it was a dog under the table, he kicked her, and the blow broke the arm of the troll's daughter.

Toward evening, the good man's daughter thought it was time for her to go home. But some of the people at the banquet ran after her, so she took off her ring and threw it behind her, and while they were all looking for it, she got up on her horse and rode away from the castle. When she arrived home, she took off her clothes by the birch tree, tied her horse there, and hastened to her usual place in the ashes beside the fire.

The man and the troll came home a short time later.

"Oh you miserable wretch," the troll said. "You don't know what fine times we've had at the palace. The prince carried my daughter about. But the poor thing fell and broke her arm."

The girl knew full well the truth of the matter, but she sat by the stove and said nothing.

The next day, they were again invited to the king's banquet.

"Hey, old man," said the troll. "Get on your clothes, and take our child to the feast. I will give the other girl some work, to help her pass the time."

When they had gone, the troll threw a bowl of flax seed among the ashes and said, "If you do not get this sorted out and all the seed back into the bowl, I shall eat you!"

The girl wept bitterly after the troll left, but then she went to her mother's grave, took the branch, and used it to strike the ashes crosswise. Instantly, all the flax seeds flew into the bowl. Then she returned to the tree, and washed herself on one side of it, dried herself on the other, and inside the tree she found clothes and jewels even finer than before. The marvelous horse appeared before her, and she rode quickly to the palace, where the king's son came out to meet her, tied her horse to a pillar, and led her into the banquet hall. At the feast, the girl sat next to him in the place of honor, as she had done the day before. But the troll's daughter sat under the table gnawing on bones, and making a terrible noise. The prince gave a kick and broke her leg.

When evening came, the good man's daughter hastened home again, throwing her golden circlet behind in order to give herself a head start. She sprang onto her horse and rode swiftly to her mother's grave. Leaving her horse and her beautiful clothes there, she hurried into the house, and when her father came home from the feast with the troll, the girl was sitting in her usual place by the hearth.

Then the troll said to her, "You wretched thing! What is there to see here compared with what we have seen at the palace? The king's son carried my daughter from one room to another—though he did let her fall, and she broke her leg."

The man's daughter said nothing, but busied herself about the hearth.

The next day, they were invited to the palace a third time. "Get up, old man! Take the little one and go ahead to the banquet. I will give the other girl work to do when we are gone."

This time she poured a bowl of milk on the ashes, saying, "If you do not get all the milk into the dish again before we get home, I will eat you up!"

The frightened girl ran to the birch tree, and by its magic power the milk flew back into the bowl. Then she washed herself on one side of the tree, dried herself on another, and dressed herself in a splendid gown and gold shoes. The same horse was there to carry her to the palace for the third time.

In the courtyard, she found the prince waiting for her. He led her into the hall, where she was seated in the place of honor. But the troll's daughter again crouched under the table, gnawing bones. Thinking it was a dog again, the prince gave a kick which knocked out her eye.

When the girl arose to leave the hall, and all those present followed after her, she threw behind her one of her golden slippers in order to get a head start. She leaped onto the horse and rode off. When she reached the birch tree, she laid aside her fine clothes and went into the house.

Scarcely was she in her usual place by the hearth when her father came home with the troll, who began to mock her, saying, "Ah, you poor stupid beast, there is nothing for you to see here—and what great things we have seen at the palace! The prince carried my little girl about again, but had the bad luck to fall and get her eye knocked out."

The girl ignored her and set about cleaning the hearth.

Now, the prince had kept all the things the girl had lost, and he made plans to find their owner. He called all the people of the kingdom to the palace for a fourth time. The troll got her daughter ready. She tied a wooden washing bat in place of her foot, a pancake roller in place of her arm, and a piece of horse-dung in place of her eye, and hurried her off to the castle.

When all the folk were gathered, the king's son said, "The maiden whose finger fits this ring, and whose head fits this circlet, and whose foot fits this slipper, shall be my bride."

Quickly the troll cut and filed her daughter's head, and finger, and foot, until they fit. And so the prince was forced to take the unseemly girl as his bride, and he went with her and her mother to their house. When it came time for him to take his horrid bride back to the palace, the girl who should have been his bride came forth from the ashes and whispered in the prince's ear, "Dear prince, do not rob me of my silver and gold."

Looking at her face, the prince recognized her at once and set off for the palace, taking both girls with him. After they had gone some little way, they came to a river, and the prince threw the troll's daughter across it as a bridge, and there she remained, unable to move.

"May a golden stalk grow from my navel, so that my mother will know me," she said. And so it happened.

Now the prince embraced the cinder lass as his bride, and they went together to her mother's grave where they received all sorts of treasures and riches—three sacks of gold and as much silver. And they went to live in the palace, and soon a son was born to them.

Word of the child's birth was brought to the man and the troll (who believed that it was her own daughter who was the baby's mother). She set out at once for the palace.

As she traveled, the troll came to the river, and began to cross the bridge, and noticed the golden reed growing up from it. She began to cut it down, in order to take it as a gift to her baby grandchild, when she heard a small voice: "Alas, mother, do not cut me."

"Is that you?" asked the troll.

"Indeed, for they threw me across the river to make a bridge of me."

In a moment the troll shattered the bridge and restored her daughter to her true form. Hastening to the palace, the troll went to the queen's bedroom and recited a magic charm,

> *Spit into my knife sheath,*
> *Bewitch my knife-blade,*
> *Become a reindeer."*

The poor queen was transformed instantly into a reindeer, and the troll used her magic to make her own daughter take on the face and form of the queen. But the baby prince missed its own mother's care and cried without ceasing.

The prince went to see a wise woman and asked, "What makes the child so restless?"

"Give the child to me," answered the wise woman. "I'll take him with me tomorrow when I drive the cows to the wood. I will make a rustling among the leaves and a trembling among the aspens. Perhaps the boy will quiet when he hears it."

"Yes, take the child to the woods with you," said the prince.

So the woman took the baby to the wood. She came to the edge of a marsh, and, seeing a herd of reindeer, she began at once to sing a magical song, and immediately one of the reindeer came and nursed the child and cared for it all day long. Then the wise woman knew that the troll had enchanted the child's real mother. She told the prince to accompany her and the baby to the woods the next day, and they built a fire by the edge of the marsh.

The reindeer came as before and began to nurse the child. "Take off your reindeer skin," said the woman, "and I will comb your hair for you." So the reindeer shed its skin, as the prince hid and watched. When the woman began combing the young queen's hair, he rushed forth at once, and seized the skin, and threw it into the fire. The queen changed into a spinning wheel, then a spindle, then into all sorts of things. But the prince smashed each one, until his own wife stood before him again, and he brought her home to the castle.

Then the prince ordered that a tub be filled with tar, and a fire lit under it, and the top covered with a blue cloth. Then he invited the troll and her daughter to take a bath in the tub, and when they stepped on the cloth, they fell into the hot tar and perished. But before they disappeared forever, the troll screamed, "May worms come upon the earth, and insects fill the air, for the torment of all humankind."

The Story of Mjadveig, Daughter of Mani

Τhis tale was collected in Iceland in the nineteenth century. Mjadveig isn't able to see through the schemes of her new stepmother, a troll, who wants to do away with her and make her own daughter look just like Mjadveig. The trolls in this story, like those in "The Magic Birch," are able to take on human form, except when eating meat. Fortunately for Mjadveig, her husband the prince has powers of his own. He can understand the language of birds and possesses a spell-dissolving plate which changes trolls back to their true, hideous shapes.

*I*t is told that in the days of yore a king named Mani governed a certain realm. He had by his queen a daughter called Mjadveig, who was distinguished in all the accomplishments that became a lady of her rank. The king built a fine and costly bower for her and surrounded her with many a maid in waiting. But it happened that the queen, her mother, fell sick and died. The king was so filled with sorrow that he kept his bed well nigh every day, taking no care of the concerns of his kingdom. So his minister, finding everything in the government going desperately wrong, advised him to seek a new wife and decided to send emissaries to find him one. But at sea they were overtaken by a strange fog, and lost their way, and knew not where they were nor whither to go. At last, they saw land and steered their ships thither.

They did not know the country, and where they put to shore, an immense wilderness lay before them. They wandered in search of human dwellings but found none. At last they heard harp playing so fine that they had heard nothing like it before, either in beauty or strangeness. They turned their steps toward the sound, until they came to a place where they saw a little tent, inwoven with silk, and in the tent sat a beautiful lady, and at her side a young girl. When the lady saw the men, she was so startled that she dropped the harp and fell into a swoon. But as soon as she had recovered, she asked them whither they were traveling. They replied that they had lost their way at sea, having been sent by King Mani in search of a wife for him, as he had lost his queen. The king's advisers found this lady very charming and asked her who she was. The lady answered their questions by telling that she had once been a queen in that land, but that an enemy had invaded and laid it to waste, and had slain the king in battle. The enemy king had intended to marry her, and to avoid him, she fled into this wilderness.

The king's advisers thought she would be a fitting match for King Mani, and at last she yielded. So she embarked with them, and a fair wind they had to the realms of King Mani. When people saw the ships approaching the shore, the king drove in his carriage down to the beach. No sooner had he caught a glimpse of his future bride than all his former sorrow was gone. Preparations were made for a grand wedding feast, which lasted a fortnight.

Now the story turns to Mjadveig, the daughter of Mani. One day the new queen came to her, saying she felt lonely at court, and invited the girl to take a walk outside the town, and the queen's daughter went with them. Now they walked, all three together, and the queen spoke kindly to her stepdaughter. But when they had gone a good way out of the town, the queen asked Mjadveig to change dresses with her daughter. So Mjadveig took off her own dress and gave it to the queen's daughter, taking hers in exchange. When this was done, the queen said, "Now do I put that charm on you, that my daughter shall so have Mjadveig's face, and look, and mien, so that no one may be able to tell one from the other."

Then the queen and her daughter bound Mjadveig hand and foot, and left her lying helpless on the ground. Then they returned to the city, and the queen put her daughter into Mjadveig's bower. The maidens of the bower thought that Mjadveig herself was there, but they found her temper rather changed by the walk.

Now Mjadveig remained in the place they had left her until she fell asleep from sorrow and despair. She dreamed that her dead mother came to her, speaking words of pity and compassion. And in the dream, her mother unbound her and gave her a cloth which would give her food, as long as she never quite emptied it or let it be seen by anyone. When Mjadveig awoke, all was as she had dreamed it.

Now it is told of the queen that she had some suspicion of Mjadveig's being alive, and therefore sent her daughter on the sly to pry about her. The girl saw Mjadveig, and saw how well she looked, and used her arts to find out how this change had been brought about.

"My mother did ill in betraying you," she said to Mjadveig. "I will share this exile with you, and we will share one and the same fate."

Mjadveig, although she distrusted the maiden's speech, was obliged to put up with this plan. After a while, the maiden lay down and pretended to fall asleep. When Mjadveig thought she was soundly napping, she moved a little way away from the sleeper, took the cloth, and began eating her meal. Now the queen's daughter had got what she wanted! She rushed up and snatched the cloth out of Mjadveig's hands and ran away homewards.

Now, Mjadveig was little better off than before. In her helplessness, she wandered about until, overpowered by weariness, she dropped off to sleep. Then she again had a dream, in which her mother came to her.

"You have acted foolishly," said her mother, "but what is done cannot be undone. Go straight down to the shore of the sea. There you will find a tongue of land that stretches out into the waves. On this tongue of land, you will find a small house, locked, but with the key in the lock. Go three times forwards and three times backwards around the house, touching the key each time as you pass by. If you do this, the house will open at the last touch of the key. There you shall dwell, and you will not find your stay weary, for

> *There cuckoos sing,*
> *There onions spring,*
> *There wethers shed their covering.*

Now Mjadveig awoke and went the way that had been pointed out to her in the dream. When she had reached the end of her journey, she found and did everything, just as her mother had bidden her. In her new abode, each day was happier than the last.

But it happened that one day she saw many fine ships sailing along the coast, steering toward the harbor. She was frightened by the sight of the ships and ran home so quickly that one of her shoes got loose, and she lost it, and this shoe of hers was of gold.

This fleet of ships belonged to a prince who had come to woo Mjadveig, daughter of Mani, to wife. When he had disembarked and started for the town, he found the delicate golden shoe, and he made a vow only to marry the lady whom this shoe would fit. Now he went to the king's palace and asked about Mjadveig, daughter of Mani. But he told them also of his vow never to marry any lady but that one whom the golden shoe should fit.

The queen asked the prince to show her the shoe, and he did so.

"Oh! I know that shoe very well," she said. "It was lost by Mjadveig, my daughter, when she was out walking."

Then she went to her daughter and took her to a room apart, and the maiden began trying the shoe on, but squeeze and thrust as much as she would, half of her foot was left out of the shoe. Finally the queen cut her daughter's heel and toes off, and so she managed to get the shoe on. Then she dressed her in finest attire and presented her to the prince, showing him that the shoe fitted.

Then the prince wooed Mjadveig (or so he thought), and he took her to his own country, saying he would come again in order to bring her family to their wedding feast.

But as his ship passed by the house of the real Mjadveig, the king's daughter, he heard a great sound of birds chirping together, and, being himself a good scholar in the language of birds, he began to pay heed now to their chirping. And the meaning of what they chirped was this,

Heel-chopped-off sits in the stern,
And full of blood is her shoe.
Here, on the sea-side
Does Mjadveig abide,
A far better bride
To woo.
Turn back then, king's son, o turn!

At first, he would not believe this bird-chatter. But then the prince took a spell-dissolving plate and put it upon his bride's shoulders, and at once she turned into a huge and ugly troll and was forced to confess her mother's evil. After this he killed her, and took the body and salted it down, the flesh filling no less than twelve barrels.

Then he rowed ashore and found the little house. The birds told him how to unlock the door, and when he had done so, he found inside a maiden of wonderful beauty and asked her name. She answered that her name was Mjadveig, and that she was the daughter of King Mani, and added that she had fled to this lonely place on account of her stepmother's cruelty.

The prince now told her his story, and what he had done with the false bride. Then he took forth the shoe and found that not only did it fit Mjadveig's foot, but that she had another golden shoe to match. With her consent, he took her on board his vessel. Leaving all his ships but one nearby, he sailed back to the king's palace and invited him, together with his queen, to his wedding feast.

Now all the king's family drove in royal carriages down to the shore and embarked and put to sea. On the voyage, the queen stayed in her cabin, so the prince went to her secretly and begged her to tell him the cause.

"My health is so poor, that I can never eat at the usual meal hours," she said. "I would appreciate it if you could find me some meat."

The prince told her that on one of his vessels there was some salt meat to be had, but that being raw, it would hardly be of any use to her. At this news, the queen brightened up and said she could easily boil it herself. She begged the prince to be silent about this matter.

Now, the truth was that whenever the queen ate, she would change into the most hideous of trolls. She ate a barrel of meat on each of the first eleven days. On the twelfth day, when she was devouring the twelfth barrel, the prince took King Mani and showed him the cannibal in her fiendish feast. When the king learned that he had been charmed by trolls, he was astonished beyond telling. They set fire to that ship so that the troll queen found a speedy end.

The prince told the king how he had found Mjadveig and took him to his daughter, and they sailed away to the prince's country, and a wedding feast was held that lasted for a month. At the end of the rejoicings, King Mani went away, honored with many gifts and precious things.

A year passed and Mjadveig was delivered of a fair male child. Some time after that, she went to bathe with one of her maidens, but when she came to the bath she wanted soap. She sent the servant home for it and waited in the bathhouse alone.

Then there came to her a woman who greeted her courteously, asking her to exchange dresses with her. This Queen Mjadveig did. Then the strange woman used magic spells to make herself look exactly like Queen Mjadveig. The true queen was charmed away and, from that very hour, vanished, and though no one knew of the change, everyone began to dislike Mjadveig.

One day it happened that the king's herdsman was walking by the seaside, and suddenly he saw a glass chamber rise up to the top of the waves, and inside it was a woman who looked exactly like Queen Mjadveig. Looped around this glass chamber was an iron chain, and the end of the chain was held by a horrid giant. After a while, the giant hauled the glass chamber back down into the waters of the sea.

The herdsman was amazed and marveled at the sight he had seen. He walked on until he came to a brook, and there he stopped in a trance of thought. While he stood there, he saw a child coming to draw water from the brook. He gave the child a gold ring. The child took the ring and disappeared into a rock that stood nearby.

Immediately afterwards, a dwarf appeared from the same rock. He thanked the herdsman for his kindness to the child and asked what he would wish him to do in return.

The herdsman begged him to explain what it was that he had seen coming up to the surface of the sea. The dwarf replied that it was Queen Mjadveig, held captive by evil trolls, and that it was the sister of the giant he had seen holding the end of the chain who had taken Mjadveig's place at the court. The giant had granted Mjadveig one wish, allowing her to come to shore four times. He had promised her that he would release her if anyone came to her rescue. "But," added the dwarf, "she has already been three times on land, and tomorrow she will come ashore for the fourth and last time."

The herdsman asked the dwarf to tell him how to release the queen. The dwarf gave him an axe and told him to cut the chain with it.

So the herdsman waited by the sea the whole night. The next day, the glass chamber came up from the waves and onto the shore, and the herdsman lost no time in using his axe and easily cut through the chain. No sooner had he done so than up rose the giant in a wild rage, ready to slay the man who had dared to break his chain. But out came the dwarf, carrying a small bag, and he flung the contents of the bag in the giant's face. This blinded the giant, and he writhed and twisted with pain, rolled over the edge of the rocks into the sea, and gave up the ghost.

They took Mjadveig to the young king, who put his magic spell-dissolving plate upon the shoulders of the supposed queen. At once she turned into an ugly giantess, who confessed what she had done to the real Mjadveig. The giant had been her brother, and the evil stepmother of Mjadveig their sister, and this had been their revenge. Then the young king had the monster shamefully killed.

The king rewarded the herdsman with wealth, and title, and a goodly share of the realm to rule over. There was then greater joy at court than words can tell.

> *Cuckoos would sing,*
> *Onions would spring,*
> *And wethers would shed their covering.*
> *And the baby prince, as he lay*
> *In his cradle kept peace, both night and day.*

Little Rag Girl

This tale was collected in the mid-nineteenth century in Georgia, a country lying between the Black Sea and the Caspian Sea, which was until recently part of the Soviet Union. The tasks given to the Little Rag Girl by her stepmother, tending a cow and spinning wool, are the kinds of work a young farm girl would have done in rural Europe a century ago and earlier. Little Rag Girl and her mean sister both meet a strange old woman who tests their kindness. This is a common happening in folktales. The two girls receive special gifts so that everyone who sees them knows what they are really like on the inside.

*T*here was and there was not, there was a miserable peasant. He had a wife and a little daughter. So poor was this peasant that his daughter was called *Conkiajgharuna*, Little Rag Girl.

Some time passed, and the man's wife died. He was unhappy before, but now a greater misfortune had befallen him. He grieved and grieved, and at last he said to himself, "I will go and take another wife. She will mind the house and tend my orphan child." And he did so, but this wife brought with her a daughter of her own. When the woman came into her husband's house and saw his child, she was angry in her heart.

She treated Little Rag Girl badly. She spoiled her own daughter, but scolded her stepdaughter and tried to get rid of her. Every day she gave her a piece of badly cooked bread and sent her out to watch the cow, saying, "Eat as much as you want, and give some to every stranger you meet, but be sure to bring the whole loaf home." The girl went away, feeling very miserable.

One day, she sat in the field and was weeping bitterly, when the cow said to her, "Why are you weeping? What is troubling you?" The girl told the cow her story, and the cow said, "Don't cry, for in one of my horns there is honey, and in the other there is butter. Take what you want."

The girl took the butter and honey, and in a short time, she grew plump. When the stepmother saw this, she flew into a rage. After that, she would give the girl a basket of wool every morning and told her to spin it all before she came home in the evening.

One day, as Little Rag Girl sat in the field spinning, the cow ran away. The girl ran after it, and as she ran, she dropped her spindle down a hole. Looking inside, she saw an old woman sitting on a stool.

"Good mother, please give me back my spindle," she said.

"I cannot, my child," the woman replied. "Come and take it yourself."

The girl went into the hole and bent down to pick up her spindle.

"Daughter, daughter, come and look at my head a moment," said the old woman. "I am almost eaten up."

The girl went and looked at her head, and she was filled with horror, for all the worms in the earth seemed to be crawling there. The little girl stroked the woman's head gently and removed some of the worms.

This pleased the old woman very much, and she said, "When you leave here, follow the road until you see three springs—one white, one black, and one yellow. Pass by the white and black, and dip your head in the yellow."

The girl did as the old woman told her. When she came to the three springs, she passed by the white and the black and bathed her head in the yellow fountain. Her hair became golden, and her hands, too, shone like gold.

When her stepmother saw this, a fury siezed her. The next day, she sent her own daughter out to tend the cow, hoping that the same good fortune would visit her.

The stepsister sat and spun, and the cow ran away as it had the day before, and the girl ran after it. She dropped her spindle down the same hole and, looking inside, she saw the old woman.

"Dog of an old woman," the stepsister cried. "Come here and give me my spindle!"

"I am not able, child," the old woman answered. "Come and take it yourself."

And when the girl came near, the old woman said, "Come, child, and look at my head." The girl came and looked at her head.

"Ugh! What a horrid head you have, you disgusting old woman!"

"Thank you, my child. I have a reward for you. When you take the road home, you will pass by three springs—a yellow, a white, and a black. Pass by the yellow and the white and dip your head in the black one."

The girl did as the old woman said; she passed by the yellow and white springs and put her head into the black. Then a long black horn grew out of her forehead. She cut it off again and again with her knife, but it grew back, longer and uglier, each time she did.

The girl ran crying to her mother, who swore that it was the cow's fault and made plans to kill the animal.

The cow knew what the stepmother wanted to do, so it went to the Little Rag girl and said, "When I am dead, gather my bones together and bury them in the earth. Whenever you are in trouble, come to my grave, and cry aloud, 'Bring my steed and my royal robes!'"

Little Rag Girl did exactly as the cow had told her. When the stepmother had killed the animal, she took its bones and buried them in the earth.

After this, some time passed. One holiday, the stepmother took her daughter to church. She placed a trough in front of Little Rag Girl, and then she spread a hundred pounds of millet around the courtyard.

"Before we return from church, fill this trough with your tears, and gather up every single grain of millet," the stepmother told her.

Little Rag girl sat down and began to weep. While she sat crying, a neighbor woman came by and asked her what was the matter. The girl told her the whole story. The woman then brought all her hens and chicks, and they picked up every grain of millet. Then she put a lump of salt in the trough and poured water over it.

"There, child," said she, "These are your tears. Now, go and enjoy yourself."

Little Rag Girl thought of the cow. She went to its grave, and said, "Bring me my steed and my royal robes." At once there appeared a horse, and beautiful clothes, and slippers of gold. Little Rag Girl put on the clothes, mounted the horse, and rode to church.

How the people stared when they saw her! Her stepsister whispered to her mother, "This girl looks very much like our own Rag Girl." The woman smiled scornfully and said, "Who would give that sun-darkener such beautiful clothes?"

Little Rag Girl left the church before anyone else. On the way home, as she was leaping over a stream, one of her golden slippers fell into the water. She arrived home and dressed once again in her rags.

A long time passed. One day, when the king's horses were drinking at that same stream, they saw something shining in the water and were frightened. The king sent his servants to find out what it was that gave the horses such a fright, and they brought him the golden slipper. When the king saw how lovely it was, he commanded his viziers to go and find its owner. "I will marry no one else," the king said.

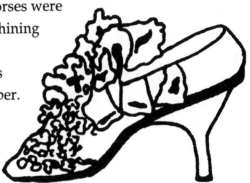

Little Rag Girl's stepmother heard this, and she dressed her own daughter in great finery and told the king that she had a daughter who was exactly the model for the shoe. But before the king arrived, she made Little Rag Girl lie in a corner and put a big basket on top of her.

When the king came into the house, he sat down on the basket, in order to try the slipper on the stepsister. As soon as he sat down, Little Rag Girl took a needle and stuck the king through the basket. He cried out, and jumped up, and asked the stepmother what she had under that basket.

"It's only a turkey I have there," she replied.

The king sat down on the basket again, and Little Rag Girl again stuck the needle into him. The king jumped up.

"Lift the basket. I want to see what is underneath!"

"No!" pleaded the stepmother. "It's only a turkey, and it will run away."

But the king lifted the basket up, and Little Rag Girl came forth.

"This slipper is mine, and it fits me well," she said.

She sat down, and the king found that it was indeed a perfect fit. Little Rag Girl became the king's wife, and her shameless stepmother was left with a dry throat.

Vasilisa the Beautiful

*B*ecause this is an old tale from Russia, it takes place in a tzardom, not a kingdom, and the heroine marries not a prince but a tzar. And, because it is from Russia, the strange old woman who helps Vasilisa is none other than Baba Yaga, the bony-legged witch, with her iron teeth and her little hut which stands up on chicken legs and turns when you call its name, *Izbushka*. Baba Yaga controls day and night, fire, and death. Because Vasilisa has her real mother's blessing, and because she knows when *not* to ask questions, Baba Yaga sends her away with a gift that will release her from her evil stepfamily.

*I*n a certain Tzardom, across three times nine kingdoms, beyond high mountain chains, there once lived a merchant. He had been married for twelve years, but in that time there had been born to him only one child, a daughter, who, from the time she was a baby, was called Vasilisa the Beautiful. When the little girl was eight years old, her mother fell ill, and it seemed that she would die. So she called her little daughter to her, and taking a tiny wooden doll from under the blanket of the bed, put it into her hands and said,

"My little Vasilisa, my dear daughter, listen to what I say, remember well my last words, and do not fail to carry out my wishes. I am dying, and I leave you this little doll along with my blessing. There is no other doll like this in the whole world. Carry it with you always in your pocket, and never show it to anyone. Whenever evil threatens you or sorrow befalls you, go to a corner, take it from your pocket, and give it something to eat and drink. It will eat and drink a little, and then you may tell it your trouble and ask its advice, and it will tell you how to act in time of need."

So saying, she kissed her little daughter on the forehead, blessed her, and shortly afterward died.

Now after the death of his wife, the merchant sorrowed for many days, but at last he wished to marry again and began to look about him for a suitable wife, and the one he chose was a widow with two daughters of her own. So the merchant married the widow and brought her home as his wife, but the little girl soon found that her stepmother was a cold and cruel woman, who loved the merchant for the sake of his wealth and had no love for his daughter. Vasilisa was the greatest beauty in the whole village, while her own daughters were as lean and homely as two crows, and because of this all three envied and hated her. They gave her all sorts of difficult tasks to perform, so that the toil might make her thin and worn and that her face would grow ugly from the sun and wind, and they treated her so cruelly that she was left few joys in life. But little Vasilisa endured all this without complaint, and while the stepmother's two daughters grew thinner and uglier, in spite of the fact that they had no chores to do, she herself grew every day more and more beautiful.

Now the reason for this was the tiny doll. Each night, when everyone else was sound asleep, Vasilisa would get up from her bed, take the doll into a closet, lock the door, and give it something to eat and drink, then she told the doll her troubles and asked its advice.

The little doll's eyes would begin to shine like glow-worms, and it would become alive. It would eat a little food and sip a little drink, and then it would comfort her and tell her how to act. While Vasilisa slept, it would get ready all her work for the next day, so that she had only to rest in the shade and gather flowers, for the doll would have the kitchen garden weeded, and the beds of cabbage watered, and plenty of fresh water brought from the well, and the stoves heated exactly right. And besides this, the little doll told her how to use a certain herb to protect her from sunburn. All the joy in Vasilisa's life came from the tiny doll that she always carried in her pocket.

Years passed, and Vasilisa grew up and became of an age when it is good to marry. All the young men in the village, high and low, rich and poor, asked for her hand, while not one of them stopped even to look at the stepmother's two daughters, so ill-favored were they. This angered their mother still more against Vasilisa, and she replied to every suitor in the same words, "Never shall the younger be wed before the older ones!" And each time she had chased a suitor from the door, she would soothe her anger and hatred by beating her stepdaughter.

Now, there came a time when it was necessary for the merchant to leave his home and to travel to a distant Tzardom. He bade farewell to his wife and her two daughters, kissed Vasilisa, and departed. Scarcely was he out of sight of the village, though, than his wife sold his house, packed all his goods, and moved with them to a house far from town, on the edge of a wild forest. Each day, while her two daughters were working indoors, the merchant's wife would send Vasilisa on one errand or another into the forest, either to find the branch of a rare bush or to bring her flowers or berries.

Now, deep in this forest, as the stepmother knew well, there was a patch of green lawn, and on the lawn stood a little hut on hens' legs, where lived a certain Baba Yaga, an old witch grandmother. She lived alone, and no one dared go near the hut, for the witch ate people just as people eat chickens. The merchant's wife sent Vasilisa into the forest each day, hoping she might meet the old witch and be devoured. But always the girl came home safe and sound, because the little doll showed her where all the plants grew that the stepmother wanted and never let her go near the hut that stood on hens' legs.

One autumn evening the merchant's wife called the three girls to her and gave them each a task. One of her daughters was to make a piece of lace, the other to knit a pair of hose, and Vasilisa was to spin a basket of flax. Then she put out all the fires in the house except a single candle and went to sleep.

The three girls worked an hour, they worked two hours, they worked three hours, and then one of the elder daughters took up the tongs as if to straighten the candle wick—and she put out the light!

"What are we to do now?" asked her sister. "The fires are all out, there is no other light in the house, and our tasks are not done."

"We must go and fetch fire," said the first. "The only house nearby is a hut in the forest, where Baba Yaga lives. One of us must go and borrow fire from her."

"I have enough light from my steel pins," said the one who was making lace, "and I will not go."

"And I have plenty of light from my silver needles," said the other, who was knitting the hose, "and I will not go."

"You, Vasilisa," they both said, "shall go and fetch the fire, for you have neither steel pins nor silver needles and cannot see to spin your flax." They rose up, pushed Vasilisa out of the house, and locked the door, crying, "Don't come back until you have fetched the fire."

Vasilisa sat down on the doorstep, took the tiny doll from one pocket, and fed it a morsel she had saved from supper. "Eat a little, my little doll," she said, "and listen to my sorrow. I must go to the hut of the old Baba Yaga in the dark forest to borrow some fire, and I fear she will eat me. Tell me what I should do."

Then the doll's eyes began to shine like two stars and it became alive. It ate a little and said, "Do not fear, little Vasilisa. Go where you have been sent. While I am with you, no harm can come to you from the old witch."

So Vasilisa put the doll back into her pocket, crossed herself, and started out into the dark, wild forest. Whether she walked a short way or a long way, the telling is easy, but the journey was hard. The wood was very dark, and she could not help trembling from fear. Suddenly she heard the sound of a horse's hoofs, and a man on horseback galloped past her. He was dressed all in white; the horse under him was milk-white; and the harness was white, and just as he passed her it became twilight.

She went a little further, and again she heard the sound of a horse's hoofs, and there came another man on horseback galloping past her. He was dressed all in red, and the horse under him was blood-red, and its harness was red, and just as he passed her the sun rose.

That whole day Vasilisa walked, for she had lost her way. She could find no path at all in the dark wood, and she had no food to set before the little doll to make it alive.

But at evening she came all at once to the green lawn where the little hut stood on its hens' legs. The wall around the hut was made of human bones, and on its top were skulls. There was a gate in the wall, whose hinges were the bones of human feet and whose locks were jaw-bones set with sharp teeth. The sight filled Vasilisa with horror, and she stopped as still as a post buried in the ground.

As she stood there, a third man on horseback came galloping up. His face was black; he was dressed all in black; and the horse he rode was coal-black. He galloped up to the gate of the hut and disappeared there as if he had sunk through the ground, and at that moment the night came and the forest grew dark.

But it was not dark on the green lawn, for instantly the eyes of all the skulls on the wall were lighted up and shone till the place was as bright as day. When she saw this Vasilisa trembled so with fear that she could not run away.

Then suddenly the wood became full of a terrible noise; the trees began to groan, the branches to creak, and the dry leaves to rustle, and the Baba Yaga came flying from the forest. She was riding in a great iron mortar and driving it with the pestle, and as she came she swept away her trail behind her with a kitchen broom.

She rode up to the gate and said,

> *Izbushka, Izbushka,*
> *Stand the way thy mother placed thee,*
> *Turn thy back to the forest and thy face to me!*

And the little hut turned facing her and stood still. Then, smelling all around her, she cried out, "Foo! Foo! I smell a smell that is Russian. Who is here?"

Vasilisa, in a great fright, came nearer to the old woman and bowing very low, said, "It is only Vasilisa, grandmother. My stepmother's daughters sent me to you to borrow some fire."

"Well," said the witch, "I know them. But if I give you the fire, you must stay with me for a time and do some work to pay for it. If not, you will be my supper." Then she turned to the gate and shouted, "Ho! You, my solid locks, unlock! You, my stout gate, open!" Instantly the locks unlocked, the gate opened of itself, and the Baba Yaga rode in, whistling. Vasilisa entered behind her, and immediately the gate shut again, and the locks snapped tight.

When they had entered the hut the old witch threw herself down on the stove, stretched out her bony legs and said, "Come, fetch everything that is in the oven, and put it on the table at once. I am hungry." So Vasilisa ran and lighted a splinter of wood from one of the skulls on the wall and took the food from the oven and set it before her. There was enough cooked meat to feed three strong men. And she brought honey, beer, and wine from the cellar, and the Baba Yaga ate and drank everything, leaving the girl only a drop of cabbage soup, a crust of bread, and a morsel of suckling pig.

When her hunger was satisfied, the old witch grew drowsy and lay down on the stove and said, "Listen to me well, and do what I tell you. Tomorrow when I am gone, clean the yard, sweep the floor, and cook my supper. Then take a quarter of a measure of wheat from my storehouse and pick out all of the black grains and wild peas you find in it. Do all that I have told you, or else *you* will be my supper!"

Then the Baba Yaga turned toward the wall and began to snore, and when Vasilisa was sure that she was fast asleep, she took the tiny doll from her pocket, put a bit of bread and a little cabbage soup before it, and said, "There, my little doll. Eat a little, drink a little, and listen to my sorrow. Here I am in the house of the old witch, and the gate in the wall is locked, and I am afraid. She has given me a difficult task, and if I do not do all she has ordered, she will eat me tomorrow. What shall I do?"

Then the eyes of the little doll began to shine like two candles. It ate a little of the bread and drank a little of the soup and said, "Do not be afraid, Vasilisa the Beautiful. Be comforted. Say your prayers and go to sleep. The morning is wiser than the evening."

So Vasilisa trusted the little doll and was comforted. She said her prayers, lay down on the floor, and went fast asleep. When she woke next morning, very early, it was still dark. She rose and looked out of the window, and she saw that the eyes of the skulls on the wall were growing dim. As she looked, the man dressed all in white, riding the milk-white horse, galloped swiftly around the corner of the hut, leaped the wall and disappeared, and as he went, it became quite light and the flames in the eyes of the skulls flickered and went out. The old witch was in the yard. She whistled, and the great iron mortar and the pestle and the kitchen broom flew out of the hut to her. As she got into the mortar the man dressed all in red, mounted on the blood-red horse, galloped like the wind around the corner of the hut, leaped the wall and was gone, and at that moment the sun rose. Then the Baba Yaga shouted, "Ho! You, my solid locks, unlock! You, my stout gate, open!" And the locks unlocked, and the gate opened, and she rode away in the mortar, driving with the pestle and sweeping away her path behind her with the broom.

When Vasilisa found herself left alone, she examined the hut, wondering to find it filled with such an abundance of everything. Then she stood still, remembering all the work that she had been told to do and wondering what to begin first. But as she looked, she rubbed her eyes, for the yard was already neatly cleaned and the floors were nicely swept, and the little doll was sitting in the storehouse picking the last black grains and wild peas out of the quarter-measure of wheat.

Vasilisa ran and took the little doll in her arms. "My dearest little doll!" she cried. "You have saved me from my trouble! Now I have only to cook the Baba Yaga's supper, since all the rest of the tasks are done."

"Cook it, with God's help," said the doll, "and then rest, and may the cooking make you healthy!" And so saying, it crept into her pocket and became again only a little wooden doll.

So Vasilisa rested all day and was refreshed, and when evening approached, she laid the table for the old witch's supper and sat looking out of the window, waiting for her coming. After a while she heard the sound of horse's hoofs and the man in black, on the coal-black horse, galloped up to the wall gate and disappeared like a great dark shadow, and instantly it became quite dark, and the eyes of all the skulls began to glitter and shine.

Then all at once the trees of the forest began to creak and groan and the leaves and the bushes to moan and sigh, and the Baba Yaga came riding out of the dark wood in the huge iron mortar, driving with the pestle and sweeping out the trail behind her with the kitchen broom. Vasilisa let her in, and the witch, smelling all around her, asked, "Well, have you done perfectly all the tasks I gave you to do, or am I to eat you for my supper?"

"Be so good as to look for yourself, grandmother," answered Vasilisa.

The Baba Yaga went all about the place, tapping with her iron pestle, and carefully examining everything. But the little doll had done its work so well that, try as hard as she might, she could not find anything to complain of. There was not a weed left in the yard, nor a speck of dust on the floors, nor a single black grain or wild pea in the wheat.

The old witch was greatly angered but was obliged to pretend to be pleased. "Well," she said, "you have done well." Then, clapping her hands, she shouted, "Ho! My faithful servants, friends of my heart! Haste and grind my wheat!" Immediately three pairs of hands appeared, seized the measure of wheat, and carried it away.

The Baba Yaga sat down to supper, and Vasilisa put before her all the food from the oven, with honey, beer, and wine. The witch ate it, bones and all, almost to the last morsel (enough for four strong men) and then, growing drowsy, stretched her bony legs on the stove and said, "Tomorrow do as you have done today, and besides those tasks, take from my storehouse a half-measure of poppy seeds and clean them one by one. Someone has mixed earth with them to annoy me and to anger me, and I must have them made perfectly clean." So saying, she turned to the wall and soon began to snore.

When she was fast asleep, Vasilisa went into the corner, took the little doll from her pocket, and set before it a part of the food that was left and asked its advice. And the doll, when it had become alive, and eaten a little food and sipped a little drink, said, "Don't worry, beautiful Vasilisa! Just do as you did last night—say your prayers and go to sleep." So Vasilisa was comforted. She said her prayers and went to sleep and did not wake till next morning when she heard the old witch in the yard whistling. She ran to the window just in time to see her take her place in the big iron mortar, and as she did so the man dressed all in red, riding on the blood-red horse, leaped over the wall and was gone, just as the sun rose over the wild forest.

As it had happened on the first morning, so it happened now. When Vasilisa looked she found that the little doll had finished all the tasks excepting the cooking of the supper. The yard was swept and in order, the floors were clean as new wood, and there was not a grain of earth left in the half-measure of poppy seeds. She rested and re-freshed herself till the afternoon, when she cooked the supper, and when evening came she laid the table and sat down to wait for the old witch's coming.

Soon the man in black, on the coal-black horse, galloped up to the gate, and the dark fell, and the eyes of the skulls began to glow. Then the ground began to quake, and the trees of the forest began to creak and the dry leaves to rustle, and the Baba Yaga came riding in her iron mortar, driving with her pestle and sweeping away her path with her broom.

When she came in, she smelled around her and went all about the hut, tapping with the pestle, but try as she might, again she could see no reason to find fault with Vasilisa's work, and she was angrier than ever. She clapped her hands and shouted,

"Ho, my trusty servants! Friends of my soul! Haste and press the oil out of my poppy-seeds!" And instantly the three pairs of hands appeared, seized the measure of poppy seeds and carried it away.

Presently the old witch sat down to supper and Vasilisa brought all she had cooked (enough for five grown men) and set it before her, and brought beer and honey, and then she herself stood silently waiting. The Baba Yaga ate and drank it all, every morsel, leaving not so much as a crumb of bread. Then she said, "Well, why are you so quiet?"

"I was afraid to speak," Vasilisa answered. "But if you will allow me, grandmother, I would like to ask you some questions."

"Well," said the witch, "just remember that every question does not lead to good. If you know too much, you will grow old too soon. What will you ask?"

"I would like to ask you," said Vasilisa, "about the men on horseback. When I came to your hut, a rider passed me. He was dressed all in white and he rode a milk-white horse. Who was he?"

"That was my white, bright day," answered the Baba Yaga angrily. "He is a servant of mine, but he cannot hurt you. Ask me more."

"Afterwards," said Vasilisa, "a second rider overtook me. He was dressed in red, and the horse he rode was blood-red. Who was he?"

"That was my servant, the round, red sun," answered the Baba Yaga, "and he, too, cannot injure you." She ground her teeth. "Ask me more," she said.

"A third rider," said Vasilisa, "came galloping up to the gate. He was black, his clothes were black, and the horse was coal-black. Who was he?"

"That was my servant, the black, dark night," answered the old witch furiously, "but he also cannot harm you. Ask me more."

But Vasilisa, remembering what the Baba Yaga had said, was silent.

"Ask me more!" cried the witch. "Why don't you ask me more? Ask me about the three pairs of hands!"

But Vasilisa saw how she snarled at her and she answered, "The three questions are enough for me. As you have said, grandmother, I would grow old too soon for asking too many questions."

"It is well for you," said the Baba Yaga, "that you did not ask about what you saw inside, but only of what you saw outside this hut. If you had asked about them, the three pair of hands would have seized you also, as they did the wheat and poppy seeds, to be my food. Now I would ask a question of you in return. How is it that you have been able to do all the tasks I gave you?"

Vasilisa was so frightened to see how the old witch ground her teeth that she almost told her about the little doll. But she thought better of it just in time and answered, "The blessing of my dead mother helps me."

Then the Baba Yaga sprang up in a fury. "Get out of my house this instant!" she shrieked. "I want no one who bears a blessing to cross my threshold! Be gone!"

Vasilisa ran to the yard, and behind her she heard the old witch shouting to the locks and the gate. The locks opened, the gate swung wide, and she ran out onto the lawn. The Baba Yaga seized from the wall one of the skulls with burning eyes and flung it after her.

"There," she howled, "is the fire for your stepmother's daughters! Take it! That is what they sent you here for, and may they have the joy of it!"

Vasilisa put the skull on the end of a stick and darted away through the forest, running as fast as she could, finding her path by the skull's glowing eyes, which went out only when morning came.

Whether she ran a long way or a short way, and whether the road was smooth or rough, towards evening of the next day, when the eyes in the skull were beginning to glimmer, she came out of the dark, wild forest to her stepmother's house.

When she came near to the gate, she thought, "Surely, by this time they will have found some fire," and threw the skull into the hedge. But it spoke to her: "Do not throw me away, beautiful Vasilisa, but take me to your stepmother."

So, looking at the house and seeing no spark of light in any of the windows, she took up the skull again and carried it with her.

Now since Vasilisa had gone, the stepmother and her two daughters had had neither fire nor light in all the house. When they struck flint and steel, the tinder would not catch, and the fire they brought from the neighbors would go out immediately as soon as they carried it over the threshhold, so that they had been unable to light or warm themselves or to cook food to eat. Therefore now, for the first time in her life, Vasilisa found herself welcomed. They opened the door to her, and the stepmother rejoiced that the light in the skull did not go out as soon as it was brought in. "Perhaps the witch's fire will stay," she said, and took the skull into the best room, set it on a candlestick, and called her two daughters to admire it.

But the eyes of the skull suddenly began to glimmer and to glow like red coals, and wherever the three turned or ran the eyes followed them, growing larger and brighter till they flamed like two furnaces, hotter and hotter till the merchant's wife and her two wicked daughters caught fire and were burned to ashes. Only Vasilisa the Beautiful was not touched.

In the morning, Vasilisa dug a deep hole in the ground and buried the skull. Then she locked the house and set out to the village, where she went to live with an old woman who was poor and childless, and there she remained, waiting for her father's return from the far-distant Tzardom.

But Vasilisa soon tired of doing nothing, and one day she said to the old woman, "It is dull for me, grandmother, to sit idly hour by hour. My hands want work to do. Please go and buy me some flax, the best and finest to be found anywhere, so that I may spin."

The old woman hastened and bought some flax of the best sort, and Vasilisa sat down to work. So well did she spin that the thread came out as even and fine as a hair, and presently there was enough to begin to weave. But so fine was the thread that no frame could be found to weave it upon, nor would any weaver undertake to make one.

Then Vasilisa went to her closet, took the little doll from her pocket, set food and drink before it, and asked its help. And after it had eaten a little and drunk a little, the doll became alive and said, "Bring me an old frame and an old basket and some hairs from a horse's mane, and I will arrange everything for you."

Vasilisa hastened to fetch all the doll had asked for and when evening came, said her prayers, went to sleep, and in the morning she found a frame, perfectly made, to weave her fine thread upon.

She wove one month, she wove two months—all the winter Vasilisa sat weaving, weaving her fine thread till the whole piece of linen was done; it was of a texture so fine that it could be passed, like thread, through the eye of a needle. When the spring came, she bleached it, so white that no snow could be compared with it. Then she said to the old woman, "Take the linen to the market, grandmother, and sell it, and the money will help pay you for my food and lodging."

When the old woman examined the linen, she said, "Never will I sell such marvelous cloth in the marketplace. No one should wear this but the Tzar himself, and tomorrow I shall carry it to the palace."

The next day, she went to the Tzar's splendid palace and began to walk up and down, up and down, beneath the windows. The servants came to ask her what she wanted, but she did not answer and kept walking up and down. At length the Tzar opened his window and asked, "What do you want, old woman?"

"O Your Majesty!" the old woman answered, "I have with me a marvelous piece of linen, and so wondrously woven I will show it to no one but you."

The Tzar bade them bring her before him and when he saw the linen, he gazed in wonder at its softness and beauty. "How much will you take for it?" he asked.

"No amount of money can buy it," she answered, "but I have brought it to you as a gift."

The Tzar could not thank her enough. He took the linen and sent her home with many rich presents. Seamstresses were called to make shirts for him out of the cloth, but when it was cut, it was so fine that none of them could hold onto it to sew it. So at last the Tzar sent for the old woman and said, "If you know how to spin such thread and weave such linen, surely you must also know how to sew shirts from it as well."

And the old woman answered, "O Your Majesty, it was not I who wove the linen. This is the work of a young woman who lives with me and is like a daughter to me."

"Then take the cloth to her," the Tzar commanded, "and ask her to make me a shirt."

The old woman brought the linen to Vasilisa and told her of the Tzar's command. Vasilisa locked herself in her room and began to make the shirts. So fast and well did she work that soon a dozen were ready. Then the old woman carried them to the Tzar, while Vasilisa washed her face, dressed her hair, put on her best gown, and sat at the window to see what would happen. Presently a servant came from the palace. "The Tzar, our lord, desires to see the clever needlewoman who has made his shirts, and to reward her with his own hands.

Vasilisa rose and went at once to the palace, and as soon as the Tzar saw her, he fell in love with her with all his soul. He took her by her hand and made her sit beside him. "Beautiful maiden," he said, "never will I part from you, and you shall be my wife."

So the Tzar and Vasilisa the Beautiful were married, and her father returned from the far-distant kingdom, and he and the old woman lived always with her in the splendid palace, in all joy and contentment. And as for the little wooden doll, Vasilisa carried it about with her in her pocket all her life.

The Little Red Fish and the Clog of Gold

The Cinderella of this tale from Iraq begs her father to marry a neighbor woman who is kind to her. When this happens in a Cinderella tale, the new stepmother is always two-faced: nice to the girl before the wedding, but cruel afterwards. The inner goodness of the heroine in this story is a magical force strong enough to overcome her stepmother's attempts to kill her on her wedding day. Notice how in this tale the storyteller offers advice and words of wisdom to the audience. Unfortunately, it is not known who the storyteller was, or when the tale was collected.

Neither here nor there lived a man, a fisherman. His wife had drowned in the great river and left him a pretty little girl no more than two years old. In a house nearby lived a widow and her daughter. The woman began to come to the fisherman's house to care for the girl and comb her hair, and every time she said to the child, "Am I not like a mother to you?" She tried to please the fisherman, but he always said, "I shall never marry. Stepmothers hate their husband's children even though their rivals are dead and buried." When his daughter grew old enough to pity him when she saw him washing his own clothes, she began to say, "Why don't you marry our neighbor, father? There is no evil in her, and she loves me as much as her own daughter."

They say water will wear away stone. In the end, the fisherman married the widow, and she came to live in his house. The wedding week was not yet over when sure enough, she began to feel jealous of her husband's daughter. She saw how much her father loved the child and indulged her. And she could not help but see that the child was fair, and quick, while her own daughter was thin and sallow, and so clumsy she did not know how to sew the seam of her gown.

No sooner did the woman feel that she was mistress of the house than she began to leave all the work for the girl to do. She would not give her stepchild soap to wash her hair and feet, and she fed her nothing but crusts and crumbs. All this the girl bore patiently, saying not a word. For she did not wish to grieve her father, and she thought, "I picked up the scorpion with my own hand; I'll save myself with my own mind."

Besides her other errands, the fisherman's daughter had to go down to the river each day to bring home her father's catch, the fish they ate and sold. One day, from beneath a basket load of three catfish, suddenly one little red fish spoke to her,

> *Child with such patience to endure,*
> *I beg you now, my life secure.*
> *Throw me back into the water,*
> *And now and always be my daughter.*

The girl stopped to listen, half in wonder and half in fear. Then retracing her steps, she flung the fish into the river and said, "Go! People say, 'Do a good deed for, even if it is like throwing gold into the sea, in God's sight it is not lost.'" And lifting itself on the face of the water, the little fish replied:

Your kindness is not in vain—
A new mother do you gain.
Come to me when you are sad,
And I shall help to make you glad.

The girl went back to the house and gave the three catfish to her stepmother. When the fisherman returned and asked about the fourth, she told him, "Father, the red fish dropped from my basket. It may have fallen into the river, for I couldn't find it again." "Never mind," he said, "it was a very small fish." But her stepmother began to scold. "You never told me there were four fishes. You never said that you lost one. Go now and look for it, before I curse you!"

It was past sunset and the girl had to walk back to the river in the dark. Her eyes swollen with tears, she stood on the water's edge and called out,

Red fish, my mother and nurse,
Come quickly and ward off a curse.

And there at her feet appeared the little red fish to comfort her and say, "Though patience is bitter, its fruit is very sweet. Now bend down and take this gold piece from my mouth. Give it to your stepmother, and she will say nothing to you." Which is exactly what happened.

The years came and the years went, and in the fisherman's house life continued as before. Nothing changed except that the two little girls were now young women.

One day a great man, the master of the merchants' guild, announced that his daughter was to be married. It was the custom for the women to gather at the bride's house on the "day of the bride's henna" to celebrate and sing as they watched the girl's feet, palms, and arms being decorated for the wedding with red henna stain. Then every mother brought her unwed daughters to be seen by the mothers of sons. Many a girl's destiny was decided on such a day.

The fisherman's wife rubbed and scrubbed her daughter and dressed her in her finest gown and hurried her off to the master merchant's house with the rest. The fisherman's daughter was left at home to fill the water jar and sweep the floor while they were gone.

But as soon as the two women were out of sight, the fisherman's daughter gathered up her gown and ran down to the river to tell the little red fish her sorrow. "You shall go to the bride's henna and sit on the cushions in the center of the hall," said the little red fish. She gave the girl a small bundle and said, "Here is everything you need to wear, with a comb of pearl for your hair and clogs of gold for your feet. But one thing you must remember: be sure to leave before your stepmother rises to go."

When the girl loosened the cloth that was knotted round the clothes, out fell a gown of silk as green as clover. It was stitched with threads and sequins of gold, and from its folds rose a sweet smell like the essence of roses. Quickly she washed herself and decked herself and tucked the comb of pearl behind her braid and slipped the golden clogs onto her feet and went tripping off to the feast.

The women from every house in the town were there. They paused in their talk to admire her face and her grace, and they thought, "This must be the governor's daughter!" They brought her sherbet and cakes made with almonds and honey and they sat her in the place of honor in the middle of them all. She looked for her stepmother with her daughter and saw them far off, near the door where the peasants were sitting, and the wives of weavers and peddlers.

Her stepmother stared at her and said to herself, "O Allah Whom we praise, how much this lady resembles my husband's daughter! But then, don't they say, 'Every seven men were made from one clod of clay'?" And the stepmother never knew that it was her very own husband's daughter and none other!

Now to spin out our tale, before the rest of the women stood up, the fisherman's daughter went to the mother of the bride to say, "May it be with God's blessings and bounty, O my aunt!" and hurried out. The sun had set and darkness was falling. On her way the girl had to cross a bridge over the stream that flowed into the king's garden. And by fate and divine decree, it happened that as she ran over the bridge one of her golden clogs fell off her foot and into the river below. It was too far to climb down to the water and search in the dusk; what if her stepmother should return home before her? So the girl took off her other shoe, and pulling her cloak around her head, dashed on her way.

When she reached the house she shed her fine clothes, rolled the pearly comb and golden clog inside them, and hid them under the woodpile. She rubbed her head and hands and feet with earth to make them dirty, and she was standing with her broom when her stepmother found her. The wife looked into her face and examined her hands and feet and said, "Still sweeping after sunset? Or are you hoping to sweep our lives away?"

What of the golden clog? Well, the current carried it into the king's garden and rolled it and rolled it until it came to rest in the pool where the king's son led his stallion to drink. Next day the prince was watering the horse. He saw that every time it lowered its head to drink, something made it shy and step back. What could there be at the bottom of the pool to frighten his stallion? He called the groom, and from the mud the man brought him the shining clog of gold.

When the prince held the beautiful little thing in his hand, he began to imagine the beautiful little foot that had worn it. He walked back to the palace with his heart busy and his mind full of the girl who owned so precious a shoe. The queen saw him lost in thought and said, "May Allah send us good news; why so careworn, my son?" "Yammah, Mother, I want you to find me a wife!" said the prince. "So much thought over one wife and no more?" said the queen. "I'll find you a thousand if you wish! I'll bring every girl in the kingdom to be your wife if you want! But tell me, my son, who is the girl who has stolen your reason?" "I want to marry the girl who owns this clog," replied the prince, and he told his mother how he had found it. "You shall have her, my son," said the queen. "I shall begin my search tomorrow as soon as it is light, and I shall not stop till I find her."

The very next day the prince's mother went to work, in at one house and out at the next with the golden clog tucked under her arm. Wherever she saw a young woman, she measured the shoe against the sole of the maiden's foot. Meanwhile the prince sat in the palace gate waiting for her return. "What news, Mother?" he asked. And she said, "Nothing yet, my son. Be patient, child, put snow on your breast and cool your passion. I'll find her yet."

And so the search continued. Entering at one gate and leaving at the next, the queen visited the houses of the nobles and the merchants and the goldsmiths. She saw the daughters of the craftsmen and the tradesmen. She went into the huts of the water carriers and the weavers, and stopped at each house until only the fishermen's hovels on the bank of the river were left. Every evening when the prince asked for news, she said, "I'll find her. I'll find her."

When the fisherfolk were told that the queen was coming to visit their houses, that wily fisherman's wife got busy. She bathed her daughter and dressed her in her best, she rinsed her hair with henna and rimmed her eyes with kohl and rubbed her cheeks till they glowed red. But still when the girl stood beside the fisherman's daughter, it was like a candle in the sun. Much as the stepchild had been ill-treated and starved, through the will of Allah and with the help of the little red fish, she had grown in beauty from day to day. Now her stepmother dragged her out of the house and into the yard. She pushed her into the bakehouse and covered its mouth with the round clay tray on which she spread her dough. This she held down with the stone of her handmill. "Don't dare move until I come for you!" said the stepmother. What could the poor girl do but crouch in the ashes and trust in Allah to save her?

When the queen arrived, the stepmother pushed her daughter forward, saying, "Kiss the hands of the prince's mother, ignorant child!" As she had done in the other houses, the queen set the girl beside her and held up her foot and measured the golden clog against it. Just at that moment the neighbor's rooster flew into the yard and began to crow,

> Ki-ki-ki-kow!
> Let the king's wife know
> They put the ugly one on show
> And hid the beauty down below!
> Ki-ki-ki-kow!

He began with his piercing cry, and the stepmother raced out and flapped her arms to chase him away. But the queen had heard the words, and she sent her servants to search both high and low. When they pushed aside the cover off the mouth of the oven, they found the girl—fair as the moon in the midst of the ashes. They brought her to the queen, and the golden clog fit as if it had been the mold from which her foot was cast.

The queen was satisfied. She said, "From this hour that daughter of yours is betrothed to my son. Make ready for the wedding. God willing, the procession shall come for her on Friday." And she gave the stepmother a purse filled with gold.

When the woman realized that her plans had failed, that her husband's daughter was to marry the prince while her own remained in the house, she was filled with anger and rage. "I'll see that he sends her back before the night is out," she said.

She took the purse of gold, ran to the perfumer's bazaar, and asked for a purge so strong that it would shred the bowels to tatters. At the sight of the gold, the perfumer began to mix the powders in his tray. Then she asked for arsenic and lime, which weaken the hair and make it fall, and an ointment that smelled like carrion.

Now the stepmother prepared the bride for her wedding. She washed her hair with henna mixed with arsenic and lime, and spread the foul ointment over her hair. Then she held the girl by her ear and poured the purge down her throat. Soon the wedding procession arrived, with horses and drums, fluttering bright clothes, and the sounds of merriment. They lifted the bride onto the litter and took her away. She came to the palace preceded by music and followed by singing and chanting and clapping of hands. She entered the chamber, the prince lifted the veil off her face, and she shone like a fourteen-day moon. A scent of amber and roses made the prince press his face into her hair. He ran his fingers over her locks, and it was like a man playing with cloth of gold. Now the bride began to feel a heaviness in her belly, but from under the hem of her gown there fell gold pieces in thousands till the carpet and the cushions were covered with gold.

Meanwhile the stepmother waited in her doorway, saying, "Now they'll bring her back in disgrace. Now she'll come back all filthy and bald." But though she stood in the doorway till dawn, from the palace no one came.

The news of the prince's fair wife began to fill the town, and the master merchant's son said to his mother, "They say that the prince's bride has a sister. I want her for my bride." Going to the fisherman's hut, his mother gave the fisherman's wife a purse full of gold and said, "Prepare the bride, for we shall come for her on Friday if God wills." And the fisherman's wife said to herself, "If what I did for my husband's daughter turned her hair to threads of gold and her belly to a fountain of coins, shall I not do the same for my own child?" She hastened to the perfumer and asked for the same powders and drugs, but stronger than before. Then she prepared her child, and the wedding procession came. When the merchant's son lifted her veil, it was like lifting the cover off a grave. The stink was so strong that it choked him, and her hair came away in his hands. So they wrapped the poor bride in her own filth and carried her back to her mother.

As for the prince, he lived with the fisherman's daughter in great happiness and joy, and God blessed them with seven children like seven golden birds.

Mulberry, mulberry,
So ends my story.
If my house were not so far
I'd bring you figs and raisins in a jar.

Nomi and the Magic Fish

This African tale was written down in 1969 by Phumla M'bane, a fifteen-year-old young woman of the Zulu people of South Africa. This is one of the few Cinderella stories recorded in Africa. It is not like any one other Cinderella tale, yet parts of it resemble tales from as far away as Germany ("Little One-eye, Little Two-eyes, and Little Three-eyes") and China ("Yeh-hsien"). Nomi's naughty tattle-tale dog is different from pets in other Cinderella tales who are faithful and helpful even after death.

When Nomi was a little girl, her mother died, and her father married another woman. This woman had a daughter called Nomsa. Nomi was a beautiful, tall child, but Nomsa was very short and ugly.

The second wife did not like Nomi. Often she beat her and sent her to bed without supper. Ever since the girl was six years old, she had sent her to the veld to look after the cattle.

Every morning, she said, "Nomi, drive the cattle to the veld. Do not come home at midday, for I have no food for you. And take your ugly dog with you. I have no bones to give it."

One day at midday, Nomi drove the animals to a deep pool to drink. In this pool, she had often seen a big fish swimming about.

The poor girl was very hungry. She sat down beside the pool and cried. Her faithful dog put his head on her arm and barked.

Soon the fish swam to her. She was afraid and wanted to run away, but the fish said, "Do not be afraid, Nomi. I shall not touch you. Why are you crying?"

The poor girl said, "I am hungry. My father's second wife is very cruel to me. Often she gives me no food to eat. This morning before breakfast she sent me to the veld with the cattle. Last night I had no supper. To her daughter she gives much food. Look at my arms. They are very thin. My fingers look like the claws of a bird. In winter I am cold. I have no warm coat to wear. Look at these ugly clothes I am wearing. I have no pretty clothes."

The fish said, "Poor child, I cannot give you pretty clothes to wear, for the wicked woman would take them away and give them to her ugly little daughter. But I can give you food to eat. Bring the cattle to this pool at midday every day."

The fish gave the hungry girl some bread and milk, and to the dog it gave a big bone full of meat.

Soon, Nomi grew fat. She looked happy and beautiful. The dog, too, was fat and did not creep under the table. They did not eat the food the wicked woman gave them. She was angry and asked, "Why do you not eat your supper at night? Why are you so fat? You say you are not hungry. Where do you get food to eat?"

She beat her with a big stick, but Nomi would not tell her who gave her the food. Then the cruel woman beat the dog. At last the poor animal said, "A big fish that lives in a deep pool in the river gives us food every day."

The girl ran to the pool and told the fish. It said, "I know the wicked woman will kill and eat me. Do not cry but take my bones and throw them into the chief's garden. Do not let anyone see you doing this."

The next day, the wicked woman did not get up. She said to her husband, "I am very, very ill. If I do not have fish to eat, I shall die. You will find a big fish in the deep pool in the river."

The man went to the pool and caught the fish. He cooked it and gave it to his wife who ate everything except the bones. These she left on her plate. She said, "Nomi, take this plate and wash it. Now, nobody will give you food to eat, you naughty girl. Take the cattle and go to the veld. There is no food for you and your ugly dog today. You will soon be thin and ugly again with fingers like the claws of a bird."

The girl hid the bones under her dress, and that night when it was dark and everyone was sleeping, she crept out of the hut. She went to the chief's garden and threw the fish bones into the garden.

The next morning the chief was walking in the garden when he saw the white bones. He sent a servant to fetch them, but every time the man tried to pick them up they fell through his fingers. The chief sent another servant to try, but he soon came back and said:

"I cannot pick them up. Every time I try, they fall through my fingers."

The Chief was angry and said:

"I shall pick them up myself!"

He tried and tried, but he could not pick them up.

At last he said: "I shall marry the girl who brings the bones to me."

All the girls of the village put on their beautiful clothes and went to the Great Place, for that was what the chief's house was called. One by one, they tried to pick up the bones which always fell through their fingers. When all the girls had tried, the chief asked:

"Are all the girls of the village here?"

One woman said, "Nomi is not here. She is on the veld looking after some cattle."

Nomsa's mother said, "Nomi is not strong. She is very thin and cannot pick up the bones."

But the Chief said, "Send a servant to fetch her."

When Nomi reached the garden, she picked up the bones easily and carried them to the chief. Her dog ran barking behind her.

The chief was very happy when he saw the beautiful girl and said, "Tomorrow, I shall marry you."

Many women stamped mealies and made big loaves of bread. The men killed six oxen and many sheep, and the next day there was a great feast. Nomsa and her mother didn't come to the feast. They were afraid and ran away into the forest.

How the Cowherd Found a Bride

This male Cinderella story was recorded in Bengal, India, in the nineteenth century. Only a careful reading will reveal the many ways in which it is like other Cinderella tales. Look for the following elements that are like those in other stories in this book: mistreatment by family, food-giving cow, magic tree, falling in love through finding a golden object (a hair, not a shoe!), helpful animals, and marriage of the hero to a person of royal status.

Once upon a time there were two brothers who were very poor and lived only by begging and gleaning. One day at harvest time they went out to glean. On their way they came to a stream with muddy banks, and in the mud a cow had stuck fast and was unable to get out. The young brother proposed that they should help it out, but the elder brother objected, saying they might be accused of theft. The younger brother persisted and so they pulled the cow out of the mud. The cow followed them home and shortly afterwards produced a calf.

In a few years the cow and her descendants multiplied in a marvelous manner so that the brothers became rich by selling the milk. They became so rich that the elder brother was able to marry. He lived at home with his wife, and the younger brother lived in the jungle grazing the cattle. The elder brother's son went every day to take his uncle's dinner to the jungle. This was not necessary, for the cow used to supply her master with all sorts of delicious food to eat. When his nephew brought out the rice, the younger brother would give the boy some of the sweets that the cow gave him and told him not to tell his parents about this and not to take any home.

But one day the boy hid some of the sweets and took them home and showed them to his mother. His mother had never seen such sweets before and thought her brother-in-law wished to poison her son. The next day, she took the dinner to him herself, and after he had eaten, she said she would comb his hair, so he put his head on her lap. As she combed his hair, he fell asleep. When she saw that he was asleep, the woman took out a knife and cut off his head. Then she got up, leaving the head and body lying there. But the cow had seen what happened, and with her horns she pushed the head along until it joined the neck, and the man immediately came to life again.

The younger brother drove his herd of cattle to a distant part of the jungle and let them take their midday rest at the foot of a bodhi tree. One day, the bodhi tree spoke to the cowherd, saying, "If you pour milk every day at my roots, you will receive a boon." The cowherd poured milk each day upon the roots of the tree, and after some time, he saw a crack in the ground. He imagined that the roots of the tree were cracking the earth, but in truth there was a snake buried there, and as it increased in size from drinking the milk, it made the ground split.

One day, the snake suddenly came forth from the crack. The cowherd was filled with terror. He was sure that the snake would devour him.But the snake said, "Do not fear! I was imprisoned in the underworld, and you have rescued me. To show my gratitude, I will grant you any wish."

The cowherd answered that the snake should choose what he would give him, and so the snake bade him come closer and breathed on the cowherd's long hair. The hair became glistening like gold!

"Your golden hair will obtain you a wife," said the snake. "In addition, you will become a very powerful man, and whatever you say will come true."

The cowherd asked him what sort of things would come true, and the snake answered, "If you say a creature shall die, it will die, and if you say it shall come to life, it will come to life. But you must not tell this to anyone, not even your wife when you marry. If you do, the power will vanish."

Some time later, it happened that the cowherd was bathing in the river, and as he bathed, one of his hairs came out, and he had a fancy to wrap it in a leaf and set it afloat on the current. Lower down on the river, a princess was bathing with her attendants, and they saw the leaf come floating by and tried to stop it. But it floated straight to the princess, and she took it, and opened it, and found the hair inside. It shone like gold, and when they measured it, it was twelve fathoms long. So the princess tied it up in a cloth and went home, and shut herself in her room, and would neither eat nor drink nor speak to anyone. Her mother sent two of her companions to find out what was the matter, and at last she told them that she would not eat or leave her chamber until they found the person to whom the golden hair belonged. If it were the hair of a man, he should be her husband.

When the Raja and Rani heard this, they sent messengers upstream to search for the owner of the golden hair. The messengers followed the banks of the stream and asked in all the villages, and they questioned everyone they met in order to find the golden-haired one. But their search was in vain and without news. Then, holy men were sent forth to search, but they also returned unsuccessful.

Then the princess said, "If you cannot find the owner of the golden hair, I will hang myself!" At this, her parrot and her tame crow said to her, "You will never be able to find the man with the golden hair. He lives in the depths of the forest, and we alone can fetch him for you. Unfasten our chains, and we will go in search of him."

The Raja ordered that the birds be unchained, and he gave them a good meal before starting. Then the crow and the parrot flew out the window, and rose into the air, and followed the river, until at last they spied the cowherd, resting with his cattle under the bodhi tree. Down they flew, and settled on the trees branches, and consulted as to how they could lure him to the palace. They decided that the crow should fly down and carry off the cowherd's flute, which was lying on the ground. So the crow pounced on the flute and carried it off in its beak. When the cowherd saw this, he ran after the crow to recover his flute, and the crow tempted him on by just fluttering from tree to tree. The cowherd kept following, and when the crow was tired, the parrot took the flute from him. Thus they led the cowherd to the city, and into the Raja's palace, and at last to the chamber of the princess, where they dropped the flute into her hand.

The cowherd asked the princess to return his flute, but she said that she would only give it to him if he promised to marry her. He was surprised and asked how she could wish to marry him when she had just seen him for the first time and they had never been betrothed.

"Do you remember one day tying a hair in a leaf and setting it afloat on the river?" she asked him. "Well, that hair has been the go-between that has arranged our betrothal."

Then the cowherd remembered how the snake had told him that his hair would find him a wife, and he asked to see the hair that the princess had found. She brought it out, and they found that it was long and bright and was indeed his.

"We belong to each other," he said.

The princess called for the door to be opened, and brought the cowherd to her father and mother, and told them that her heart's desire was fulfilled. If they did not allow the wedding, she told them, she would run away with the cowherd.

So a day was fixed for the wedding, and they were married. The cowherd soon became so much in love with his bride that he forgot all about his herd of cattle, which he had left behind without anyone to look after them. So he told the princess that he must return to his cattle, whether she came with him or not. She said that she would take leave of her parents and go with him. Then the Raja gave them a feast, and handed over half of his kingdom to the cowherd, and gave him a son's share of his elephants, and horses, and flocks and herds, and said to him, "You are free to do as you like. You can stay here, or go to your own home. But if you decide to stay here, I will never turn you out."

The cowherd thought about this and decided he would live with his father-in-law. But first, he would go and take care of the cattle that he had abandoned without anyone to look after them. So the next day, he and the princess set off. When they reached the jungle they found that all the cattle were lying dead. At this, the cowherd was filled with grief and began to weep—but then he remembered the promise of the snake. He gathered herbs and held them under the noses of the dead animals, pretending that it was medicine. "Come to life," he whispered. And behold, one by one the cows all got up and began lowing to their calves. In gratitude to the snake, the cowherd filled a large vessel with milk and poured it at the foot of the bodhi tree. The snake came out and breathed on the hair of the princess, and it too became as bright as gold.

They next day they collected the cows and drove them back to the princess's home. The cowherd and his wife lived happily there, ruling half the kingdom.

After some years, the cowherd reflected that the snake had been a father and mother to him, and yet he had never taken a proper farewell of the creature. So he set forth to see if it was still there. But he could not find it. In vain he spoke to the bodhi tree, but there was no answer, and he had to return home disappointed.

The Invisible One

This tale was recorded in the mid-nineteenth century from a Native American storyteller of the Micmac people of eastern Canada. Oochigeaskw, mistreated by her sisters, goes forth wearing a dress made of tree bark, like Katie Woodencloak in the Norwegian tale in this collection. But her future husband is no mere human prince. He is an invisible supernatural being; the storyteller called him a "moose spirit." The heroines of Cinderella tales usually pass a test of some kind—patience, kindness, skill in spinning or sewing, for example—but Oochigeaskw passes a different kind of test, a test of seeing what other young women do not.

*T*here was once a large Indian village situated on the border of a lake. At the end of the village was a lodge, in which there dwelt a young man who was always invisible. His sister attended to his wants, and it was known that any girl who could see him might marry him. There were few young women who did not try, but it was long before one succeeded.

And it would happen like this—towards evening, when the Invisible One was supposed to be returning home, his sister would walk with any girls who came down to the shore of the lake. She could always see her brother, since to her he was always visible. When he appeared to her, she would say to her companions, "Do you see my brother?"

And they they would usually answer yes, though some would say no. And then the sister would ask, "Of what is his shoulder-strap made?" But as some tell the tale, she would ask other things as well, such as, "With what does he draw his sled?" And they would reply, "A strip of rawhide," of "A green withe," or something of the kind. And then she would know they had not told the truth, that they did not see him. "Let us return to the wigwam," she would say.

And when they entered that place, she would bid them not to take a certain seat, for it was his. And after they had helped to cook the supper, they would wait with great curiousity to see him eat. Truly, he gave proof that he was a real person, for as he took off his moccasins they became visible, and his sister hung them up. But beyond this, they beheld nothing, not even when they remained all night, as many did.

There lived in the village an old man, a widower, with three daughters. The youngest of these was very small and weak, and was often ill, which did not prevent her sisters, especially the eldest, from treating her with great cruelty. The second daughter was kinder, and sometimes took the part of the poor abused little girl, but the other would burn her hands and face with hot coals. Her whole body was scarred with the marks made by this torture, so that people called her *Oochigeaskw*, the burnt-face girl. And when her father, coming home, asked what it meant that the child was so disfigured, her sister would promptly say that it was the fault of the girl herself, for, having been forbidden to go near the fire, she had disobeyed and fallen in.

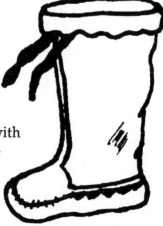

Now it came to pass that it entered the heads of the two elder sisters that they would go and try their fortune at seeing the Invisible One. So they dressed themselves in their finest and strove to look their fairest, and finding his sister at home, they went with her to take the usual walk down to the water.

Then, when her brother came, being asked if they saw him, they said "certainly." And they replied to the question of the shoulder strap or sled cord, "A piece of rawhide." In saying that, they lied like the rest, for they had seen nothing.

When their father returned home the next evening, he brought with him many of the pretty little shells from which wampum was made, and they were soon engaged in stringing the beads.

The next day, Oochigeaskw, the burnt-faced girl, who always ran barefoot, got a pair of her father's old moccasins. She begged her sisters for a few wampum shells. The eldest called her a lying little pest, but the other gave her a few. And so, dressed in only a few rags, the poor girl went out and got from the woods a few sheets of bark, from which she made a dress, putting some drawings on the bark. Thus she made a petticoat and a loose gown, a cap, leggings, and handkerchief, and, having put on her father's great old moccasins—which came nearly up to her knees—she went forth to try her luck. Truly her luck had a most inauspicious beginning, for there was one long storm of ridicule and hisses, yells and hoots, from her own door to the house of the Invisible One. But she went on, for she was greatly resolved.

Now this poor small creature in strange attire, with her hair singed off and her little face as full of burns and scars as there are holes in a sieve, was, for all this, most kindly received by the sister of the Invisible One. That noble girl knew more than the mere outside of things as the world knows them. And as the evening sky became black, she took the little burnt-faced girl down to the lake. Before long, they knew he had come. "Do you see him?" the sister asked.

"Truly I do, and he is wonderful," the girl replied.

"And what is his sled string?"

"It is the rainbow!" replied the burnt-face girl.

"But my sister," said the other, "what is his bow-string?"

"His bowstring is the Milky Way."

"You have seen him," said the sister. And taking the girl home, she bathed her. And as she washed her, all the scars disappeared from her face and her body. The sister of the Invisible One combed her hair, and as she combed her hair, it grew, and it was very long, and it was like a blackbird's wing. Her eyes shone like stars. In all the world, there was no such beauty. The sister of the Invisible One gave her a wedding garment, and bade her take the wife's seat in the lodge.

And when the Invisible one entered, terrible and beautiful, he smiled and said, "Truly you see me." "Yes," was her reply. So she became his wife.

Poor Turkey Girl

This Native American tale was recorded at Zuni, New Mexico, in the late nineteenth century. Many features of the tale are like Charles Perrault's Cinderella, such as the helpful birds, the beautiful clothes, the important dance, and the warning to the Turkey Girl not to stay too late. What would have happened if Perrault's Cinderella had not left the ball when the clock struck midnight? Turkey Girl finds out. The teller of "Poor Turkey Girl" connects the tale to a familiar part of the local landscape, markings like turkey tracks on a canyon wall.

Long, long ago, our ancients had neither sheep nor horses nor cattle, yet they did have domestic animals of various kinds, and among them, turkeys.

In Matsaki, or the Salt City, lived many very wealthy families, who possessed large flocks of these birds. It was their custom to have their slaves or the poor people of the town tend the birds in the plains round about Thunder Mountain and on the mesas beyond.

Now, in Matsaki at this time there stood, away out near the border of the town, a little tumbledown, single-room house, and a very poor girl—so poor that her clothes were patched and tattered and dirty—lived there alone. And though her person was shameful to look upon because of long neglect and bad food, she had a winning face and bright eyes. So poor was she that she herded turkeys for a living, and little was given to her except the food she subsisted on from day to day, and perhaps now and then a piece of old, worn-out clothing.

Like the extremely poor everywhere and at all times, she was humble, and her longing for kindness, which she never received, made her kind even to the creatures that depended upon her. She lavished kindness upon the turkeys she drove to and from the plains every day. In return, the turkeys were very obedient. They loved their mistress so much that at her call they would do whatever she wished.

One day, she was driving her turkeys down into the plains near Old Zuñi—the Middle Ant Hill of the World, as our ancients have taught us to call our home—and as she went along she heard the herald-priest proclaiming from the house-top that the Dance of the Sacred Bird would take place in four days.

This poor girl had never been allowed to join in or even to watch this dance, and she longed to go. But she put aside her longing, saying, "It is impossible that I should watch, much less join in the Dance of the Sacred Bird. I am ugly and shabby." Talking half to herself, half to her turkeys, she drove them on, and at night returned them to their cages at the edge of town.

Every day, she saw people preparing their garments for the dance, and cooking delicacies, and otherwise making ready for the festival, and talking and laughing merrily. As the girl went about with her turkeys each day, she would tell them of her secret wish, though she never dreamed that they understood a word of what she was saying.

On the fourth day, after the people of Matsaki had all departed toward Zuñi, the girl was wandering around the plains alone with her turkeys, and one of the big gobblers strutted up to her. He made a fan of his tail and skirts and wings, and, puffed with importance, stretched out his neck and said, "Maiden mother, we know what your thoughts are, and truly we pity you. We wish that you could go to this dance, like the other people in Matsaki. We have said this to each other at night, after you have placed us in our cages. Now listen well. If you will bring us in early this afternoon, when the dance is most gay and the people most happy, we will dress you so prettily that never a man, woman, or child will know you. But rather, the young men will wonder whence you came and long to lay hold of your hand in the circle that forms round the altar. Maiden mother, would you like to go to see this dance, and even to join in it, and be merry with the best of your people?"

The girl was surprised at first. But then, it seemed natural to her that the turkeys should talk to her as she did to them, so she sat down on a little mound and said, "My beloved turkeys, how happy I am that we may speak together! But why should you tell me of things that you know I cannot do?"

"Trust in us," said the old gobbler, "When we begin to call and call and gobble and gobble, and turn toward our home in Matsaki, follow us and we will show you what we can do for you. Only listen. No one knows how much happiness and good fortune may come to you if you enjoy moderately the pleasures of the dance. But if, in your enjoyment, you should forget us, who are your friends yet depend so much upon you, then we will think that you deserve this hard life of yours after all."

"Never fear, my turkeys," cried the maiden. "In everything you tell me to do I will be obedient as you always have been to me."

The sun had scarcely begun to decline when the turkeys turned homeward of their own accord. The maiden followed them, light of heart. When all had entered their cages, the old gobbler bade her to enter his house, and she went in.

"Now maiden, sit down," said he, "and give me your old clothes."

The maiden obediently drew off the ragged mantle that covered her shoulders and cast it on the ground before him. He seized it in his beak, and spread it out, and pecked at it, and, lowering his wings, began to strut back and forth over it. When he laid it down at the feet of the maiden, it had become a beautiful white embroidered cotton mantle. Then another turkey came forth, and she gave him another garment, and then another, and another, until each was as new and beautiful as any possessed by the maidens of Matsaki. The turkeys circled about her, singing and singing, clucking and clucking, brushing her with their wings, until she was clean, and fair, and bright, and her eyes were dancing with smiles.

Finally, an old turkey came forward and said, "Now you lack only beautiful jewelry. We turkeys have keen eyes, and over the years have gathered many valuable objects, small and precious."

Spreading his wings, he danced round and round, throwing his head back, and, beginning to cough, he produced in his beak a beautiful necklace, and another turkey brought forth earrings, and so on, until all the proper ornaments befitting a young maiden appeared and were laid at the feet of the poor turkey girl.

She decorated herself with these beautiful things and, thanking the turkeys over and over, set off for Zuñi.

"O maiden mother, leave open the gate, for who knows whether you will remember your turkeys when your fortunes have changed. You may grow ashamed that you have been the maiden mother of turkeys. But we love you and would bring you good fortune. Remember therefore our words of advice and do not stay too long at the dance."

"I will surely remember, O my turkeys!" answered the maiden.

Hastily she sped away down the river path toward Zuñi. When she arrived, she went in at the western side of the town, through one of the long covered ways that led into the dance court. When she came just inside of the court, behold, everyone began to look at her, and many murmurs ran through the crowd, murmurs of astonishment at her beauty and at the richness of her dress. The people were all asking one another, "Who is this beautiful maiden?"

She was invited to join the youths and maidens dancing round the center of the plaza. With a blush and a smile and a toss of her hair over her eyes, the maiden stepped into the circle, and the finest youths among the dancers vied with one another for her hand. Her heart became light and her feet merry, and the music sped her breath to rapid coming and going, and the warmth swept over her face, and she danced and danced until the sun sank low in the west.

But alas! She did not think of her turkeys, or, if she thought of them, she said to herself, "Why should I leave all this for my flock of gobbling turkeys? I will stay a while longer, and just before the sun sets I will run back to them."

So the time sped on, and another dance was called, and another, and never a moment did the people let her rest. The would have her in every dance as they moved around the musicians and the altar in the center of the plaza.

At last the sun set, and the dance was nearly over, when suddenly the girl broke away and ran out and sped up the river path before anyone could follow the course she had taken.

Meanwhile, as it grew late, the turkeys began to wonder why their maiden mother did not return to them. At last a gray old gobbler mournfully exclaimed, "It is as we might have expected. She has forgotten us. She is not worth of better things than those she has been accustomed to. Let us go into the mountains, and be captives no more, since our maiden mother is not as good and true as we once thought."

So they trooped out of their cages and ran up toward the canyon of the cottonwoods, and then round behind Thunder Mountain, through the Gateway of Zuñi, and up the valley.

All breathless, the maiden arrived at the open gate of the cage and looked in. Not a turkey was there! She ran up the valley, hoping to overtake them, but they were far ahead. It was only after a long time that she came within the sound of their voices and heard them singing this song,

> *K'yaanaa, to! to!*
> *K'yaanaa, to! to!*
> *Ye ye!*
> *K'yaanaa, to! to!*
> *K'yaanaa, to! to!*
> *Yee huli huli!*
> *Hon awen Tsita*
> *Itiwanakwin*
> *Otakyaan aaa kyaa;*
> *Lesna Akyaaa*
> *Shoya-k'oskwi*
> *Teyathltokwin*
> *Hon aawani!*
> *Ye yee huli huli,*
> *Tot-tot, tot-tot, tot-tot,*

Huli huli!
Up the river, to! to!
Up the river, to! to!
Sing ye ye!
Up the river, to! to!
the river, to! to!
Sing ye huli huli!
Oh our maiden mother
To the middle place
To dance went away;
Therefore as she lingers,
To the Canyon Mesa
And the plains above it
We all run away!
Sing ye ye huli huli,
Tot-tot, tot-tot, tot-tot,
Huli huli!
Tot-tot, tot-tot, tot-tot,
Huli huli!

Hearing this, the maiden called to her turkeys, and called and called in vain. They only quickened their steps, spreading their wings to help them along, singing the song over and over until they came to the base of Canyon Mesa, at the borders of the Zuñi Mountains. Then singing once more their song, they spread wide their wings and *thlaswa-a-a, thlakwa-a-a,* they fluttered away over the plains.

The girl looked down at her dress. It was changed to what it had been, and she was the same poor turkey girl that she had been before. Weary, grieving, and despairing, she returned to Matsaki.

Thus it was in the days of the ancients. On the rocks leading up to the top of Canyon Mesa are the tracks of turkeys, and other figures can also be seen. The latter are the song that the turkeys sang, graven in the rocks. Since that day, all over the plains along the borders of Zuñi Mountains, turkeys have been more abundant than in any other place.

The gods dispose of men according as men are fitted. If the poor be poor in heart and spirit as well as in appearance, how will they be anything but poor to the end of their days?

Ashpet

The story of Ashpet was recorded in the 1940s in the Appalachian mountain region of Virginia from a descendant of settlers from Europe. Ashpet is a servant in the house of a cruel woman and her two daughters—she is not a stepdaughter. As in many Cinderella tales, Ashpet's troubles are not over after her wedding. The two daughters pretend to be her friends, then push her into the river at a spot near the Hairy Man's cave. The Hairy Man is a creature something like a giant or a devil who is featured in many folktales from the American south. Fairy tales brought to the United States from Europe are often told as if they happened in America, while keeping kings, queens, princes, and princesses as characters.

*O*ne time there was a woman had two daughters, and they kept a hired girl. They treated this girl mean. She was bound out to 'em, had to do all the hard work, little as she was. They wouldn't buy her any pretty clothes or nothin'. Made her sleep right up against the fireplace and the ashes got all over her, so they called her Ashpet.

Well, one day they were all fixin' to go to church-meetin'. They never let Ashpet anywhere. They knew she was prettier than the old woman's two girls, and if anybody came to the house they always shoved Ashpet under a washtub. That day, just when they were tryin' to get fixed up to go to meetin', their fire went out, so they had to borrow fire. Now there was an old witch-woman lived over the gap in the mountain. These rich folks, they wouldn't have nothin' to do with this old woman but they had to have fire so they sent the oldest one of the girls over there to borrow some fire. The oldest girl she went traipsin' on over the gap. She thought herself so good she didn't go in the house, just stuck her hand through a crack in the logs.

"I come after fire."

"Come in and comb my hair and I'll give ye some."

"I'll not put my pretty clean hands on your old cat-comb!"

"You'll get no fire."

The old woman she sent the next-oldest. She went a-swishin' up the hill and through the gap. She was so nice! She ran her hand through that crack.

"I want some fire."

"Come in and comb my hair."

"Me? Put my nice white hands on your old cat-comb?"

"Put off then. You'll get no fire."

Then the old woman hollered for Ashpet. And Ashpet she went on up through the gap, ran down the holler, and went right on in the house.

"Good evenin', Auntie."

"Good evenin', Ashpet."

"I want to borry a coal of fire, please, ma'm."

"Comb my hair and you can have it."

Ashpet combed her hair for her, and then the old woman gave her some fire—put a hot coal inside an old dried toadstool.

"You goin' to meetin', Ashpet?"

"Law, no! They never let me go anywhere at all. I got to wash the dishes and scour the pots. I'll not get done till meetin's plumb over."

"You want to go?"

"Why, yes, I'd like that the best in the world."

"Time they all get good and gone, I'll be up there to see you."

Ashpet she ran on back over the mountain and built up the fires, got in wood and water, and went to milkin' and feedin'. She had to hurry 'cause she had supper to cook, too. Then they ate supper, and Ashpet helped the two girls get fixed up, and finally they all went on off to meetin'. When they were all out of sight down the road here came that old witch-woman a-hobblin' through the gap with her stick. She walked in the house, went on out to the kitchen, says to Ashpet, says, "You just keep right still there by the door now."

So Ashpet looked in the kitchen door; and the old woman set all the dishes on one end of the table and the dishpan on the other end and hit full of scaldin' water. Then she knocked on the table, says,

> *All dirty dishes stay off the shelf!*
> *Get in the water, shake yourself!*
> *Wash, dish! Wash!*

And the plates and platters and cups and saucers and bowls and knives and forks and spoons ran over and slipped through the hot water and rose up and shook themselves and hopped up on the shelves just as clean and dry as anybody'd have to do in an hour's hard work. Then the old woman she opened the back door, says,

> *Pots and skillets—handle and spout!*
> *Get in the sand and scour out!*
> *Scrub, pot! Scrub!*

And it was a sight in the world how every pot and pan and kettle and skillet went hoppin' and straddlin' out the door and rolled down to the creek and went to rubbin' and scrapin' in the sand and dippin' in the water, and then they all came bumpin' back in the house and settled down by the hearthrock right where they belonged. Ashpet had an awful good time watchin' all that. She nearly laughed herself to death.

Then the old woman reached in her apron pocket, took out a mouse, and an old piece of leather and a rawhide string, two scraps of shoe-leather, and an old piece of rag. She put the mouse down before the door, laid that chunk of leather on it, dropped that rawhide string over its head, says,

> *Co-up, little mare!*
> *Whoa now! Whoa!*

—and there stood the finest little pied-ed mare you ever saw—pretty new saddle and bridle on it, and it was just as gentle as a girl 'uld want. Then that old witch-woman she knocked that piece of rag around this way and that, laid it on the bed; took the two scraps of leather, knocked them up a time or two, set 'em under the bed, says, "Now, Ashpet, you shut your eyes and wish for the dress and slippers you want to wear to meetin'."

Ashpet shut her eyes and wished and when she opened 'em there was a pretty red dress stretched out on the coverlet, and under the bed were the prettiest red slippers—the littlest 'uns you ever saw. Then Ashpet she washed herself and put on her red dress and slippers.

"Now," says the old woman, "quick as meetin' breaks, you get back here and hide your horse in the bresh, and hide your dress and slippers, and put on your old ashy clothes again."

Ashpet went ridin' on up to the church-house, and tied her horse and walked in the door. Everybody saw her, but nobody knew who she was. Now the king's son was there and he kept his eyes right on her. When meetin' started breakin' he followed Ashpet, and saw her get on her little mare and turn its head to go, so he jumped on his horse and took out after her. She paid no attention, but he caught up with her directly, started talkin' to her.

They rode on a piece, and then she eased off one of her slippers and kicked it in the bresh; rode on a little piece farther, says, "I've lost one of my slippers, sure's the world! It must have dropped off in the road somewhere between here and the church-house."

"I'll get it for you," he told her. "You wait here now." And he turned his horse and went back. But time he was out of sight, she galloped her little mare on home, hid it in the woods, ran to the house and hid her dress and slipper, got her old ashy dress again and went to sweepin' and dustin'.

That boy had a time findin' her slipper but fin'lly he saw it there in the bresh, picked it up, and when he rode on back and found the girl gone he didn't know what in the world to do.

Well, he took that little red slipper and went all over the country lookin' for the one it would fit. Got down there where the old woman and the two girls lived at fin'lly; and when they saw him comin', they grabbed Ashpet and run with her and stuck her under that wash-tub.

The king's son came on in with the slipper, says, "This slipper came off the prettiest woman in the world, and the one it fits is the one I'll marry."

The oldest 'un she took the slipper and ran out behind the house; took a knife and trimmed her heel and her toes till she made it fit. The boy looked at her other foot and he got suspicious; and just about that time a little bird flew to the door and started singin':

Trim your heels, and trim your toes!
Under the tub the slipper goes!

"What did you say, little bird?"

"Shoo!" says the old woman, and the bird flew off.

The king's son he jerked the slipper off that girl and he saw how she'd trimmed her heel and her toes. So the next-oldest she grabbed up the slipper and ran out. She squeezed her foot in it, but she had to trim her heel and toes, too. Then that boy he looked at her foot and it was in the slipper all right but when he looked at her face he wasn't satisfied at all; so he pulled the slipper off again and then he noticed where she had been trimmin' her heel and toes.

Then that little bird fluttered at the door again—

Trim your heels! Trim your toes!
Under the tub the slipper goes!

"SHOO!" hollered the old woman.

But the king's son he watched the bird and it flew out in the yard and lit on that tub—

Trim your heels! Trim your toes!
Under the tub the slipper goes!

So the boy went out and lifted the tub and looked in under it, and there was Ashpet.

"What you doin' under there?"

"They always put me under here."

"Come on out."

"I'm too ragged and dirty."

"You try this slipper on. Here!"

So Ashpet stuck out her foot, and he put the slipper on it, and it fitted perfect. Then she went and washed her face and put on her red dress and her other slipper; ran out in the bresh and got her horse, and she and the king's son rode on off and got married.

Well, the two girls and the old woman they acted awful nice after the weddin', went up to the king's house several times and they always brought Ashpet somethin'. Then one day the girls told her about a fine place to go swimmin', says, "Let's go up there today and go in. Come on and go with us, Ashpet."

So they took Ashpet up to the swimmin' place and both the girls acted like they were goin' in the water but they let Ashpet go in first. They knew that an Old Hairy Man lived in that

132

hole of water; and when Ashpet went in, he got her. The two girls laughed and went on home.

The Old Hairy Man kept Ashpet in a cave in the bank over that deep water, and she couldn't get away from him. There wasn't any boat, and the water was swift and it licked right up to the mouth of the cave. Well, after Ashpet was there a day or so the Old Hairy Man got to braggin' about how his hide was so thick there couldn't no ball nor bullet hurt him.

"Can't hurt ye nowhere?" Ashpet asked him.

"Nowhere," he told her, "—except a little mole back of my left shoulder. If I was to get hit there it 'uld lay me out, cold."

Now the king's son had done raised an army to hunt for his wife, and they fin'lly came by that cave. Ashpet ran out and stood over that deep hole, and they saw her.

"Shoot him in the back of his left shoulder!" she hollered to 'em. Then she ran and hid behind a big rock.

The men they got some boats and rowed across and shot in the mouth of the cave. Here came the Old Hairy Man a-scrapin' and a-gruntin', and he went to grabbin' the men out the boats and throwin' 'em back across the river as fast as they landed, but they got more boats and landed on both sides of that cave. They kept on shootin' but the bullets and balls just glanced off the Old Hairy Man's hide, and he kept right on fightin' and a-throwin the men every which-a-way. But fin'lly the king's boy and some of his men got in behind him and they went to aimin' back of his left shoulder until one ball happened to hit that mole—and that fixed him—knocked him out, cold.

So they took Ashpet and ran for their life, rowed across in a hurry. Old Hairy Man he came to about the time they landed on the other side, and he went to jumpin' up and down a-hollerin', "You got my woman!"

Well, as soon as the king's boy got Ashpet home safe, he went and arrested that old woman and her two girls, carried 'em down to that deep hole of water and threw 'em in. Says, "Here's ye three women!"

And Old Hairy Man he came out and grabbed 'em and hauled 'em in his cave—and they're down there yet, I reckon.

Benizara and Kakezara

The story of Benizara and Kakezara was told by Japanese storyteller Tsune Watanabe in the 1960s.

Benizara, like many other Cinderellas, has an encounter with a strange and frightening old woman. In this tale, the woman is an *oni*—a Japanese ogre or demon. The beautiful dress Benizara receives is a kimono, and in it she is so lovely that she attracts the attention of a great nobleman. But it is neither by beauty nor by having her foot fit a shoe that Benizara proves that she is superior to her stepsister, Kakezara. Instead, Benizara uses a skill not found in other Cinderella tales; she is a poet!

*L*ong ago in a certain place there were two sisters. One was named Benizara, "Crimson Dish" and the other Kakezara, "Broken Dish." Benizara was a former wife's child, while Kakezara was the stepmother's child. Benizara was a very honest and gentle girl, but her stepmother was very cruel to her.

One day she sent the two girls out to gather chestnuts. She gave Benizara a bag with a hole in the bottom, but she gave Kakezara a good one. "You must not come back until you have each filled your bag," she said.

The two set off for the mountains and began to pick up chestnuts. Before long Kakezara's bag was full, and she returned home, leaving Benizara alone. Benizara was an honest girl, and so she worked as hard as she could picking up chestnuts until it began to get dark. It got darker and darker, and she thought she heard a rustling sound, *gasa gasa*, as though a wolf were coming toward her. She suddenly realized how dangerous it was and ran off without even looking where she was going. In the meantime it had become very dark, and she was completely lost. She was filled with despair, but she knew that it would do no good to cry, so she kept on walking, thinking that perhaps she might find a house. Suddenly just ahead she saw a light. She went to where it was and found an old woman alone spinning thread. Benizara explained that she had gone to gather chestnuts but that it was late and she couldn't return home. Then she asked if she might please stay overnight there.

The old woman said: "I would like to let you stay here, but both my sons are *oni*. They will soon be coming home and would eat up anyone they found here. Instead, I will tell you how to find your way home." And she carefully explained which road to take. Then she filled her bag with chestnuts and gave her a little box and a handful of rice. "Take the chestnuts to your mother. This little box is a magic box. If there is ever anything that you need, just say what you would like, then tap on the box three times and what you want will appear. Now if you meet my *oni* sons on your way home, chew some of the rice and spread it around your mouth; then lie down and pretend that you are dead."

Benizara thanked her for everything and started for home on the road she had been told to take. After a while she heard the sound of a flute coming toward her. She chewed some of the rice and spread it around her mouth, then lay down by the side of the road and pretended that she was dead. Soon a red *oni* and a blue *oni* came along.

"Hey, older brother, I smell human beings," said one and went over to the side of the road to look. "It's no good, older brother, she's already rotten. Her mouth is full of worms," he said. And they went on down the road blowing their flutes.

Benizara listened to the sound of the flutes growing fainter and fainter in the distance; then she continued on down the road that she had been told to take.

Soon morning came. At home her stepmother was thinking to herself that during the night the wolves would have surely eaten Benizara, when just then the girl arrived home. Far from being dead, she had a whole bag full of chestnuts; so the stepmother had nothing to scold her about.

One day some time after this a play was to be given in the village. The stepmother took Kakezara and went to see it, giving Benizara a great deal of work which had to be done before they returned home. Benizara was working as hard as she could, when some of her friends came and asked her to go with them to see the play. Benizara said that her stepmother had given her so much work to do that she could not go, but her friends said, "We will help you and then you can go," and so, all working together, they soon finished a whole day's work.

Her friends were all wearing beautiful kimonos, but Benizara had nothing but rags to wear. She wondered what she should do; then she thought about the little box she had received from the old woman in the mountains. She took it out and said that she would like to have a kimono. She was given a beautiful kimono. She put it on and went to see the play. When she got there, Kakezara was begging her mother for some candies and Benizara threw her some. When she did this, a nobleman who had come to see the performance of the play saw what happened.

The next day the nobleman's colorful procession came to the village. The lord's palanquin stopped in front of Benizara's house. Kakezara's mother was overjoyed and dressed Kakezara in her very best to meet him. The lord got out of the palanquin and said, "There should be two girls here; bring out the other one too."

The stepmother had put Benizara in the bath tub to hide her, but there was nothing she could do but obey the lord's command, and so she brought her out. In comparison to Kakezara, Benizara looked very shabby, but the lord said, "Which one of these two came to see the performance of the play yesterday?"

"It was this one, Kakezara."

"No, it wasn't that one," said the lord, but the mother kept insisting that it was. Finally it was decided to ask each of them to compose a song. The lord took a plate and put it on a tray; then he piled some salt in the plate and stuck a pine needle in it. He commanded that they each compose a poem, using that as a subject.

In a loud voice Kakezara sang,

> *Put a plate on a tray,*
> *Put some salt on the plate,*
> *Stick a pine needle in the salt;*
> *It'll soon fall over.*

Then she hit the lord on the head and ran off. Next Benizara sang,

> *A tray and plate, oh!*
> *A mountain rises from the plate,*
> *On it, snow has fallen.*
> *Rooted deep into the snow,*
> *A lonely pine tree grows.*

When he heard this song, the lord praised it very highly. Preparations were soon made, and Benizara was put into a beautiful palanquin; then she rode off to the lord's palace.

Kakezara's mother watched in silence; then she put Kakezara in a huge empty basket, saying, "Now, Kakezara, you too may go to the lord's palace." She dragged her along, but she did it so violently that Kakezara tumbled over the edge of a deep ditch and fell to her death.

Maria

This Filipino Cinderella tale was told in the Tagalog language to a folktale collector in 1903. The Philippines were settled by the Spanish in the sixteenth century, and this tale resembles Cinderella stories found in Spain and the Hispanic regions of North and South America—particularly the motif of the golden jewel which appears on Maria's forehead. Magic animals and a magic tree help Maria in ways that are familiar to the readers of Cinderella tales, but the *kinds* of animals and tree are native to the Philippines.

*T*here were once a man and his wife who had a very beautiful daughter named Maria. The man fell in love with a widow who had three children. One day while he and his wife were on the river in a boat, he pushed her out, and she was drowned. Then he married the other woman, who was as wicked as he. Poor Maria, with all her beauty, became the household drudge, condemned to do all the dirty work.

Maria had a pet pig who was her only companion, and one day her stepmother ordered her to kill it and clean it. Poor Maria cried and begged, but the woman ordered her to kill the animal. When the pig was cleaned, the stepmother gave Maria the entrails, and told her to wash them in the river and not to lose any of the pieces. Maria did so, but as she washed them, a piece floated off into the river. Maria cried and lamented so that an old crocodile came up out of the river and asked her what was the matter. "That is nothing," said the crocodile when she told him of her trouble. He swam after the missing piece and brought it back, and as he turned to swim away and splashed his tail, a drop of water landed on Maria's forehead, where it became a bright jewel that flashed like the sun. The girl went home with the jewel on her forehead shining so brightly that it made everyone cross-eyed to look at it, and it had to be covered with a handkerchief.

The cruel stepmother questioned Maria about her good fortune, and when she had found out everything, she sent her own daughter to kill a pig, and to do in all respects as Maria had done. But this time, when the crocodile splashed the stepsister with his tail, instead of a jewel on the girl's forehead, there was a little bell that rang incessantly. All the people laughed and pointed at her, and the bell could not be gotten off, and she was very ashamed.

The stepmother was more cruel than ever to Maria now that she had met with good fortune and her own daughter with ill. She set the girl to every kind of work until her whole body was filthy, and then sent her to the river to bathe, telling her that if there was even one speck of dirt on her back, she would beat her to death.

Maria struggled and scrubbed, but she could not reach all over her back, and she began to cry. Out of the river came a great she-crab, who asked the girl her trouble. "Oh," said Maria, "if I do not wash my back clean, my stepmother will beat me to death." "Very well," said the crab, "that is easily remedied." And jumping onto Maria's back, the crab scrubbed and scrubbed until her back was perfectly clean.

"Now," said the crab, "you must eat me and take my shell home and bury it in the yard. Something will grow up that will be valuable to you."

Maria did as she was told and from the place grew a fine grapefruit tree which in time bore one fruit.

One day, the stepmother and her daughter went to church and left Maria to fix their dinner. The stepmother told her that dinner must be ready when she returned and must be neither cold nor hot. Maria wept again over the impossible task, and was about to despair when an old woman came in and listened to the girl's troubles. The woman told Maria to go to church, and she would prepare the dinner. Maria said she could not go, for she had no fine clothes, but the old woman told her to look in the grapefruit. Maria did this, and in the fruit she found the garments of a princess and a little chariot with eight horses as well. Quickly she arrayed herself and drove to the church by way of the king's palace. The jewel shone on her forehead, and it nearly blinded all who looked upon it. The king sent his soldiers to find out who she was, but they could learn nothing and returned with only one of her little slippers which fell off as she left the church.

Maria returned home and hastily put the dress and chariot and horses back into the grapefruit, and the old woman was there waiting with the dinner, which was neither cold nor hot. When the stepmother came home from church, she saw only her stepdaughter there in rags, and everything was ready according to her orders.

Now, the king sent out a proclamation that all the women of the kingdom must try on the shoe. His soldiers went here, there, and everywhere in search of little feet, but the shoe would fit no one. At last they came to Maria's house. Now, Maria had a very small foot, while those of her stepsisters were huge, so the stepmother wrapped Maria in an old mat and put her up in the rafters, telling her not to move. The soldiers searched the house. "Surely there is someone wrapped in that mat," they said. "Oh, no," said the stepmother, "that is only a bundle of old rags." But one of the soldiers stuck the mat with the end of his sword, and Maria cried out. The soldiers then had her wash her face and were astonished at her beauty. They took her to the king, and the shoe fitted exactly. The king married her with great feasting and pomp, and they lived together happily for many years.

The Story of Tam and Cam

This story of Cam and her evil stepsister Tam was collected from a Vietnamese storyteller in the late nineteenth century. Details of this story—the fish that helps Cam, and the prince who falls in love with Cam after seeing only her shoe— are very much like parts of "Yeh-hsien," which was told in a part of China near Vietnam over a thousand years earlier. And the crow that carries Cam's shoe to the prince plays a role identical to that of the eagle in the ancient Egyptian "Rhodopis."

Tam and her mother might win a contest for the cruelest stepmother and stepsister in a Cinderella tale, and they certainly get two of the worst punishments.

A husband and wife each had a child from a first marriage. The man's daughter was named Cam, and the woman's daughter was called Tam. The two girls seemed to be about the same age, but which one deserved the privileges of the elder? The man and woman gave each girl a basket and sent them off to catch fish. The one who caught the most, they said, would have the position of elder daughter.

Cam soon caught many more fish than Tam. Tam thought of a trick. She told her sister to go to the other side of the river and pick a jasmine flower. While Cam was gone, Tam put all the fish in her own basket and ran home. Cam returned and found only one fish in her basket, a *bong mú*.

She sat down and began to cry. A spirit, moved by her sadness, came down from the sky and asked her what was wrong. She told him how her sister had stolen her fish. "Have you nothing left at all?" asked the spirit. Cam showed him the *bong mú*, and he told her to keep the fish, and feed it, and care for it.

Cam placed the *bong mú* in the well, and she would feed him each evening with rice from her own dinner. The fish learned to come when she called. He would eat, and she would tell him her sorrows. Tam was spying on her, though, and one day when Cam was out tending the water buffalos, Tam called the fish. She caught it, and cooked it, and ate it.

When Cam returned from the fields, she called to the *bong mú*, but he did not appear, and she began to cry. The rooster said, "O-o-o! Give me three grains of rice, and I'll show you his bones." Cam gave him the rice, and the rooster showed her the bones of the *bong mú* that had been thrown on the garbage heap.

Cam wept as she gathered the bones of the fish. The spirit appeared to her again and told her to buy four little pots, and put the bones into them, and to bury the four pots at the four corners of her bed. At the end of three months and ten days, she would find in the pots her heart's desire.

Cam did as she was told, and when she opened the pots after three months and ten days, she found a beautiful dress, and pants, and a pair of golden slippers. Cam wrapped the clothes in an old rag and ran out to the fields to try them on where no one could see her. But as she did so, the golden slippers became wet, and so she placed them on a rock to dry.  A crow flew down and carried off one of them and dropped it into the courtyard of the palace of the crown prince of that country. When the prince saw the delicate slipper, he announced that he would only marry the girl whose foot it would fit.

The stepmother would not let Cam go to the palace to try the slipper. She hurried off with her daughter, but they returned home, unsuccessful. Cam begged and pleaded to go try herself. The stepmother then mixed lentils and sesame seeds together. "When you have separated every last grain," she said, "then you may have my permission to go to the palace."

The spirit sent a flock of pigeons to help Cam. The birds descended from the trees, and soon they had picked up and sorted the grain. But the stepmother noticed that some were missing, and so she would not allow Cam to go. Then the pigeons coughed and coughed—and up came a few grains that were in stuck their throats, and at last the stepmother had to let Cam go to the palace. She tried on the slipper, which fit her perfectly, and the king's son took her as his bride.

One day, not long after the wedding, Cam was called home to visit her father, who was sick. As the father lay in bed, his wife had placed crisp crackers under the covers next to him, which made a breaking noise whenever he moved. The stepmother told Cam that this sound was the cracking of her poor father's bones. He was desperately ill, she said, and could only be cured by eating the fruit of a tree that grew in their garden. Cam must climb the tree and pick one of the fruits, or her father might die.

Tam sharpened the axe. As soon as Cam was up in the tree, she cut it down. Cam fell to the ground, but she did not die—she was transformed into a *quanh quach* bird.

Tam took Cam's clothes, and put them on, and presented herself at the palace. "My sister, Cam, is dead, so I have come to take her place," said Tam.

The prince was sad. Every day he missed Cam. Then one morning, as Tam washed the prince's clothes and spread them out to dry on a wall, a *quanh quach* bird landed on a tree nearby.

"Dry my husband's clothes properly," chirped the bird. "Don't let them get torn on the wall."

The prince heard the bird speak, and said, "If you are my wife, fly into my sleeve."

The *quanh quach* bird flew into the sleeve of the prince's coat. He took the bird into the palace, and fed it, and cared for it, and spoke to it tenderly. Tam was overcome with jealousy. She seized the bird, and cooked it, and ate it. When the prince found his dear bird missing, he demanded to know what had happened to it.

"I must be pregnant," Tam said. "I had such a craving for bird's meat."

"At least tell me where you have put the feathers," demanded the prince.

Tam showed him where she had thrown the feathers behind the wall. A slender bamboo shoot grew there. The prince tended and watered the plant and spoke sweet words to it.

One day when the prince was out hunting, Tam cut the bamboo shoot, and cooked it, and ate it. She threw away the bark, and from that bark sprang a durian tree. The tree grew swiftly to a great height, and it put forth one fruit which gave off a pungent and irresistible smell. Yet no one was able to climb the tree and pick its fruit.

One evening, an old beggar woman sat down beneath the tree. She smelled the fruit, and said, "O durian, could you please fall into the basket of a hungry old woman?" The fruit fell directly into her basket, and she carried it home to her tiny hut and placed it on a shelf.

The next day, when the old woman was out begging, Cam emerged from the durian fruit. She cleaned the hut and prepared dinner for the old woman, then she went back inside the fruit. The old woman was astonished when she returned home. The next morning, she only pretended to leave the hut, but instead, she hid and watched through the window and saw Cam as she emerged from the fruit and began preparing food.

"You are as a daughter to me," said the old woman. "How can I repay you?"

"Go to the palace," Cam answered, "and invite the prince to dinner."

"Why would he want to come to my miserable hut," the old woman asked.

"Please do as I ask," said Cam.

But the prince only laughed when he heard the woman's invitation. "I will come to your house," he said, "if you weave a silken carpet, embroidered with gold, that will reach from my door to yours."

With the help of the spirit, Cam wove the carpet in the space of a night, and spread it on the ground before sunrise, and so the prince came. Cam prepared a feast for him, then she hid behind a curtain. The prince looked sadly at the delicacies that lay on the old beggar woman's table. "My wife prepared food exactly this way," he said. "No other woman could do it as finely. Where is she?" Then Cam came forth from behind the curtain. The prince rewarded the old woman with gold and silver, and joyfully he took Cam back to the palace.

When Tam saw her stepsister returning with the prince, she was astonished. Cam had been a girl when she had last seen her—now she was a beautiful woman.

"How have you become so pretty?" Tam asked.

"If you wish to be as lovely as I am," Cam replied, "fill a large cauldron with boiling water, and jump in."

Tam believed her, and threw herself into boiling water, and there she perished.

Cam had Tam's flesh salted and sent to the stepmother who, believing it was pork, began to eat it. A bird in the treetop called out, "The hungry crow eats her child's flesh and cracks her bones."

"My daughter sent me this meat!" cried the stepmother angrily.

But at the bottom of the barrel, she found Tam's head, and knew that she was dead.

Glossary to the Tales

amber Translucent, fossilized resin, used to make jewelry. It gives off a subtle perfume when rubbed.

arsenic A very poisonous chemical.

bade Past tense of the verb, to bid: to ask, tell, or command.

betrothal A mutual pledge to marry.

betrothed Engaged to be married.

bodhi A tree, sacred in India.

bound out Working without pay, usually for several years, in repayment of a debt.

bower A private ladies' chamber.

breeches Trousers that reach to just below the knee.

brogues Coarse shoes of untanned leather.

bullock-traces A trail made by bulls (bullocks).

byre A cow barn.

cairn A large pile or mound of stones, often part of an ancient ruin.

carrion The decaying flesh of a dead body.

charm A chanted word, phrase, or verse that supposedly has magic power.

clog A shoe with a thick, usually wooden, sole.

clomb Archaic (old) past tense of the verb, to climb.

conceit An idea or thought.

doitherin' Foolish.

dun Brown, or grayish-brown.

emissaries Persons sent on an official mission.

entrails Intestines and/or other inner organs of an animal.

fathom The length of the two arms outstretched.

fell A treeless, rocky hill.

fen A marsh or swamp.

flax A plant, the fibers of which are spun and used to weave linen cloth.

glean To collect the remaining grain from a reaped field.

graven Carved; engraved.

gruel A thin cereal or porridge.

henwife A woman who practices magic.

henna A plant, and also the dye extracted from this plant, used to dye the hair, and also ceremonially to draw designs on the skin.

herdsman A person who tends a herd of animals.

hither To or toward this place.

hovel A small, miserable dwelling place.

kohl   A powder used as eye makeup.

last   A form, shaped like a foot, on which shoes are made.

lath   A thin, narrow strip of wood.

lentil   A small, flat, round bean.

lime   A caustic substance that quickly destroys animal or plant tissue.

linen   Thread or cloth made from flax.

lough   A bay or inlet of a sea.

mantle   A loose, sleeveless cloak or cape.

mealies   Ground millet.

mien   A person's way of acting and moving.

millet   A very small, round grain.

mortar   A hard bowl in which softer substances are pounded with a pestle.

ogress   A female ogre, a cannibalistic creature of folklore and legend.

oni   In Japanese folklore, a monster or demon.

palanquin   A covered sedan chair, carried on the shoulders of two or more men.

pestle   A rod used to grind substances in a mortar.

pied   Spotted in two or more colors.

pitch   A black, sticky substance; tar.

purge   Laxative.

rarely   Very; extremely.

reel   A spool upon which thread is wound.

rushes   Tall grasslike plants that grow in wet places. Their leaves and stems are used in weaving baskets and mats.

signify   To mean (something).

silvern   Silvery; made of silver.

spindle   A specially made, hand-held rod used for spinning fiber such as flax, cotton, or wool into thread.

spur   A ridge coming out from the side of a range of hills or mountains.

swine   Pig; pigs.

swing by the back   A wrestling match.

thither   To or toward that place.

troll   In Scandinavian folklore, a supernatural creature, usually a cannibal.

veld   Open grassland.

vizier   A government officer; minister of state.

wampum   Beads, once used by some Native American groups as money.

wan   Having a pale, sickly complexion.

wethers   Male sheep.

whither   To what place? Where?

withe   A flexible twig used for binding things.

woo   To seek in marriage.

Notes to the Tales

Notes

Rhodopis: A Cinderella in Ancient Egypt?

Strabo's great work, *Geography*, in seventeen books, was completed around 7 B.C. A later Greek writer, Aelian (170-235 A.D.), also mentioned Rhodopis in his collection of historical miscellany, *Varia Historia*, in which he identifies her as a Thracian, a fellow-slave of Aesop. Complete Cinderella-type stories based on this fragment about Rhodopis, such as the picture book *The Egyptian Cinderella*, are inauthentic.

If it is surprising to modern readers that the prince in Perrault's *Cinderella* falls in love with the heroine at first sight, it is even more surprising that in *Rhodopis* the king falls in love with the unseen owner of a shoe! This motif is used in several of the tales in this book: the Chinese "Yeh-hsien," the Vietnamese "Tam and Cam," and the Iraqi "The Little Red Fish and the Clog of Gold." This may reflect the immense physical and social distance between the heroine and her future mate, and perhaps also the seclusion of women in these societies. In the East Indian tale "How a Cowherd Found a Bride," a princess falls in love with the herdboy's one golden hair. Falling in love after seeing a picture, hearing a name spoken, or finding a golden hair, is a common theme in European fairy tales and medieval romances.

Yeh-hsien (China)

Arthur Waley. "The Chinese Cinderella Story." *Folk-Lore* 58 (1947).

The relationship between this story and Cinderella was first suggested by the Japanese folklorist K. Minakata in *Jinrui Gaku Zasshi*, XXVI (1911); *Yeh-hsien* was also a subject of R.D. Jameson's *Three Lectures on Chinese Folklore* (1932, reprinted in Alan Dundes' *Cinderella: A Folklore Casebook*).

According to Arthur Waley, a scholar and translator of Chinese literature into English, we owe the preservation of this very early tale to the Chinese official, Tuan Ch'eng-shih, who recorded it in about 850-60 A.D. Tuan wrote a book entitled *Yu Yang Tsa Tsu* (*Miscellany of Forgotten Lore*), which included many stories from the oral tradition, some from China, and some from other lands. The story of Yeh-hsien was told to Tuan by a family servant, Li Shih-yuan, who came from the caves of Yung-chou in southern China, near present-day Vietnam. The island of T'o-han is a location referred to elsewhere in Chinese history, but its modern name and exact location are unknown. The story as it appeared in Tuan's book is reprinted in Chinese characters in the children's book *Yeh-shen* by Ai-Ling Louie.

A different Chinese Cinderella tale is included in Wolfram Eberhard's *Folktales of China*, and Chinese folklorist Nai-Tung Ting discusses 21 versions of Cinderella from China in *The Cinderella Cycle in China and Indo-China*.

Cinderella, or the Little Glass Slipper (France)

From Charles Perrault's *Histoires ou contes du temps passé, aves moralités*. Translated by Judy Sierra.

The Cinderella tale that is best known in Europe and the Americas is that of Charles Perrault (1628-1703), a member of the court of Louis XIV of France. This very idiosyncratic retelling of the oral traditional tale appeared in print in 1697, in a collection entitled *Histoires ou contes du temps passé, aves moralités (Stories or Tales from Times Past, with Morals)*. Perrault published this collection of eight tales using the name of his son, Pierre d'Armancour, who was seventeen at the time. Although the tales have always been attributed to the father (Charles Perrault was a well-known author, while Pierre's name never appeared on any other writings), there is no definitive proof of authorship. Of the seven other tales in this collection, four are almost as widely known as

Cinderella: "Sleeping Beauty," "Little Red Riding Hood," "Blue Beard," and "Puss in Boots." The first English translation of the tales appeared in 1729. By 1770, the work had also been translated into German, Dutch, and Russian, and the popularity of Perrault's tales has continued to the present day.

Although Perrault based his Cinderella on oral tradition, he rewrote it for the sophisticated audience of the court at Versailles, and it differs from most oral versions in several respects. The helping role of the fairy godmother is usually played in other versions of the tale by the spirit of the dead mother, or by a helpful animal. The transformation of mice into horses, rat into coachman, lizards into lackeys, and pumpkin into coach are probably also Perrault's inventions. In her survey of 345 Cinderella texts, Marian Roalfe Cox found only six instances of slippers made of glass. Gold slippers occur much more frequently. Many writers have claimed that Cinderella's slipper should have been made of fur, and that Perrault somehow confused the french *vair* (fur) with *verre* (glass). Although this makes a good story, a fur slipper would hardly have been a fitting match for Cinderella's dress made of "cloth of silver and gold, embroidered with jewels."

Each of the eight tales included in Perrault's book had a moral in verse attached, though these are usually omitted in modern editions. Perrault took part in an intellectual battle over the comparative merit of ancient and modern writings. Perrault was on the side of the *modernes*. It is thought that one of his motives in publishing the *Contes* was to show the moral superiority of French folktales to the amoral Greek myths, thus the necessity of hitting the reader with an ethical lesson.

Before the publication of *Histoires ou contes du temps passé*, Perrault had written and published a much less successful volume of tales in verse, which included another Cinderella-type story, "Peau d'Ane." I have not included Perrault's "Peau d'Ane" in this volume, because I feel that his telling in verse is too far removed from the oral tradition. Folktales were never told in metered, rhyming verse, and the demands of meter and rhyme, I believe, demand too many changes in content. For a prose translation, see any complete collection of Perrault's tales. I have included a recent French oral version of the "Peau d'Ane" story, "Peu d'Anisso," in this collection.

Peu d'Anisso (France)

Genevieve Massignon, ed. *Folktales of France.* Translated by Jacqueline Hyland. Chicago: University of Chicago Press, 1968.

"Peu d'Anisso" is translated and edited from an oral telling in regional dialect, recorded in 1960 from the seventy-eight-year-old peasant woman, identified by the collector as the widow Delage, a native of Le Lindois living in Vitrac-Saint-Vincent (in Charente, in the west of France).

This type of Cinderella tale is characterized in French folklore by the Prince's three encounters with the heroine dressed as a servant. The Prince strikes the servant successively with three household objects—in this case, a poker, a bellows, and a *friquet* (the local name for the stick used to stir the meat to make *grillons* or potted minced pork). Aarne and Thompson classify this tale plot as tale type 510B. This tale is mentioned in French literature even before Perrault. Noel du Fail referred to *Cuir d'Asnette* (The She Donkey's Hide) in his *Propos Rustiques* (1547), and Bonaventure des Periers included the story *D'une Jeune Fille Surnommée Peau d'Asne* (A Young Girl Nicknamed "Donkey Skin") in his *Contes ou Nouvelles Récréations et Joyeux Devis* (1557).

In tales of the type 510B, the heroine's troubles originate with her father, rather than her stepmother or mother. Her father loves her too much, and he wants to marry her. She tricks him into giving her three impossibly beautiful dresses, like the sun, moon, and stars. Then, dressed in ugly, shabby clothing, she leaves home and becomes a servant in a royal or noble household. The three beautiful dresses enable her to attend three balls and become a rich man's bride.

Tales of this type have had difficulty getting through the "editorial filters" of English-language publishing for children, and when they have, the beginning is usually altered so that the heroine leaves home because her father wants her to marry someone she doesn't like. I first heard a version "Peau d'Ane" told by a French school-teacher, who found nothing unsuitable for children in its contents, yet I feel instinctively that adults in the U.S. would object if they heard me tell it to a group of children.

Another characteristic of tale type 510B is that the prince or young gentleman is very cruel to the heroine in her ugly disguise. Yet he never apologizes or makes amends for his behavior, as if it were quite natural to physically abuse the hired help. One can imagine this story being told among the servants in a wealthy household, as the young girls daydream of being magically rescued from a life of drudgery.

Aschenputtel (Germany: Jacob and Wilhelm Grimm)

From the Grimms' *Kinder und Hausmärchen*, 1857 edition. Translated by Judy Sierra.

Readers familiar with Perrault's and Disney's Cinderella are usually shocked to encounter the Grimms' "Aschenputtel," which is often given the misleading title "Cinderella" in English translation. In particular, the stepsisters' self-mutilation shocks, yet this motif is widespread in oral tradition.

The Grimms have been criticized for changes they made in their tales from the first edition (1812-25) to the last (1857). Yet "Aschenputtel" is much closer to what we know of European oral versions of Cinderella tales than is Perrault's. This is because Jacob and Wilhelm Grimm were scholars who set about collecting German folktales not as literary entertainment, but as "raw data" for their project of reconstructing pre-Christian German mythology. As researchers, they tried to record the tales exactly as they were told by traditional storytellers. However, their volumes of tales were instant best-sellers, and beginning with the second edition, Wilhelm Grimm eliminated from the collection all material he did not consider suitable for children. Grimms' fairy tales were quickly becoming standard family bedtime reading.

The assistance given to Aschenputtel by the tree on her dead mother's grave and by the birds she encounters there seems mysterious and primitive, especially in comparison to the cheerful fairy godmother of Perrault who makes house calls. According to legends and folk beliefs, fairies were not the good-natured, winged creatures of literature, but rather frightening beings, closely related to the spirits of the dead. The image of the gift-bearing tree growing on the mother's grave is central to a great many Cinderella-type stories.

The punishment of the stepsisters by birds that peck out their eyes seems to have been an invention by Wilhelm Grimm. It was not included in the first edition. Punishment of the evil stepfamily is not a part of every Cinderella tale, although when it does occur it can be most gruesome. The stepmothers in the Icelandic tale "Mjadveig, Daughter of Mani," and the Vietnamese "Tam and Cam" are both tricked into eating their daughters, for example.

For further information about changes the Grimms made in the fairy tales, see Ruth Bottigheimer's *Grimms' Bad Girls and Bold Boys*.

Allerleirauh, or the Many-furred Creature (Germany: Jacob and Wilhelm Brimm)

Andrew Lang. *The Green Fairy Book*. London: Longman's Green, 1892.

Andrew Lang (1844-1912), was the compiler of the well-known fairy books of many colors, and also a writer and folktale scholar. "Allerleirauh" is one of the Grimms' fairy tales, but it is not usually included in anthologies of their tales for children. See the note to "Peu d'Anisso," earlier, for a discussion of the suppression of this Cinderella variant in English-language children's books. Andrew Lang changed the part of the tale in which the heroine's father decides to marry her; I have restored it from the Grimms' version. In Charlotte Huck's picture book retelling of this tale, *Princess Furball*, a king orders his daugher to marry an ogre. Anita Lobel reclaims the message of the original in her illustration, where we see the ogre's portrait displayed for Princess Furball, and it looks very much like the father.

Little One-eye, Little Two-eyes, and Little Three-eyes (Germany: Jacob and Wilhelm Grimm)

Andrew Lang. *The Green Fairy Book*. London: Longman's Green, 1892.

Both Marian Roalfe Cox, in her study of Cinderella tales, and Antti Aarne and Stith Thompson, in *The Types of the Folktale*, recognized this tale's similarity to Cinderella. Cox classified it with "indeterminate" variants—a sort of miscellany of tales that resembled Cinderella, Catskin, or Cap o' Rushes in some way. Aarne and Thompson gave these tales their own tale type, 511, which immediately follows the "true" Cinderella types, 510A and 510B. The features that make this tale like Cinderella are the mistreatment by the family or stepfamily, the helpful animal, and marriage to a man of higher rank. Unlike the heroine of 510A or 510B, though, Two-eyes does not leave home or visit a dance or church. And her future husband recognizes her worth by her ability to pick the fruit of a magical tree. This tale type has been widely collected in Europe and the Middle East, and one Spanish-language version from the U.S. includes sisters with as many as *nine* eyes! Tales of this type are very similar, and so I have only included one version, that of the Grimms, in this collection.

Cap o' Rushes (England)

Joseph Jacobs. *English Folk and Fairy Tales*. New York: G.P. Putnam's, 1898.

Joseph Jacobs (1853-1916) was one of the best-known British folklorists of the nineteenth century, and he was equally distinguished as a historian. In addition to his scholarly work, he re-wrote, compiled, and published six collections of folktales for children. Like Andrew Lang's fairy books, Jacobs' collections have remained continuously in print. But unlike the long, tedious and literary texts in Lang's anthologies, Jacobs'

stories are delightfully tellable. In a biography of Jacobs, his daughter wrote that he never missed an opportunity to tell these tales to child audiences; the experience of the storyteller is evident in the retellings. Though his collections were published primarily for children, Jacobs always included a section of scholarly and comparative notes.

Jacobs cites as the source for this version of "Cap o' Rushes" the contribution of a Mrs. Walter-Thomas to the "Suffolk Notes and Queries" section of the *Ipswitch Journal* (no date given). This article was subsequently reprinted in the British journal *Folk-Lore* of September 1890. It was common at that time for amateur folklore collectors to seek out and write down the tales of traditional storytellers, and to submit them to newspapers and magazines.

The "like meat loves salt" motif in this tale is found in many areas of Europe and is an alternative to the tale opening in which the father wishes to marry his daughter. Both give the girl cause to leave home and seek her fortune. It is only in the "meat loves salt" tales that the girl and her father are reconciled at the end of the story. A British folktale of this sort is thought to be the original source of the story of *King Lear* (though the "meat loves salt" motif is not present in the play). Shakespeare's source may have been Geoffrey of Monmouths folklore-laden history of England, *Historia Regum Britanniae*, written in the twelfth century.

Billy Beg and the Bull (Ireland)

Seumas MacManus. *In Chimney Corners*. New York: Doubleday, 1899.

Seumas MacManus (1867-1960) was born in the western part of Ireland, where he grew up speaking Irish and hearing stories told by the fireside. He emigrated to the United States as a young man and had a long and successful career as a writer of fiction, poetry, and plays. His English language retellings of the Irish stories are particularly rich in language and detail.

"Billy Beg and the Bull" is typical of what is arguably termed a "male Cinderella story," featuring a mistreated ash lad. Like Billy Beg, ash lads typically become giant killers and/or dragonslayers, winning a royal mate through their valor, while female Cinderellas succeed through beauty, kindness, or simply a mysterious fate which takes their shoe to a future husband. The slipper-test ending of "Billy Beg" is unusual for a dragonslayer tale (Aarne-Thompson tale type 300), and makes it seem even more Cinderella-like. In most dragonslayer tales, the hero remains unrecognized despite his great feats. An impostor claims to have killed the dragon, but cannot produce the beast's tongue. The true hero is recognized when he produces that missing part from his pocket.

MacManus' version, "Billy Beg and the Bull," demonstrates the sort of humor a traditional Irish storyteller could express in a magical hero tale. Through the efforts of the Irish Folklore Commission, sound recordings of such storytellers were made in the early part of the twentieth century, and with these recordings it was possible to appreciate how different tellers infused tales with their own personalities.

Also evident in this tale is the Irish storytelling tradition of the "run"—a long, tongue-twisting passage that is repeated word-for-word at certain points in the story. The following are examples of runs from "Billy Beg and the Bull":

> ...where you wouldn't know day by night or night by day, over high hills, low hills, sheep-walks, and bullock-traces, the Cove of Cork, and old Tom Fox with his bugle horn.

and

> ... they knocked the soft ground into hard ground, the hard ground into soft, the soft into spring wells, the spring wells into rocks, and the rocks into high hills.

According to James Delargy, in "The Gaelic Story-Teller,"

> The main function of these embellishments is to impress the listener, and the more corrupt and unintelligible they are, the greater the effect; but they serve also as resting-places for

the storyteller in the recital of long, intricate tales, from which he can view swiftly the ground he has to cover. They are recited at a greater speed than the narrative proper.

Fair, Brown, and Trembling (Ireland)

Jeremiah Curtin. *Myths and Folk-Lore of Ireland.* Boston: Little, Brown, 1890.

Jeremiah Curtin (1840-1906) was an American linguist and folklorist who collected the oral narratives of many Native American and European storytellers. This particular tale was collected in the west of Ireland in 1887, in the Irish language, and translated into English by Curtin.

The telling of long hero tales was a highly developed tradition in Ireland, and the battle scenes that are typical of the male hero tales have made their way even into this Cinderella story in the form of the battle of the princes for the hand of Trembling. The appearance in this tale of kings and princes of both real and imaginary foreign countries is also typical of the Irish hero tale tradition. The honey-bird and honey-finger are a mystery to me.

Hearth Cat (Portugal)

Consiglieri Pedroso. *Portuguese Folk-tales.* Translated by Henriqueta Monteiro. London: The Folk-Lore Society, 1882.

Consiglieri Pedroso collected these oral tales himself and, according to his introduction to this collection, he tried to convey the storytellers' words as exactly as possible. The text of "Hearth Cat" is awkward and often confusing; however, it is so unique that I wanted to include it in this collection. I have tried to smooth out the text without changing the actual events and characters of the story.

In European folk beliefs, a well was often thought to be an entrance to a strange otherworld, the abode of fairies. This Portuguese Cinderella tale is unusual because the helpful animal, the giver of dresses, *and* the prince are one and the same being.

Katie Woodencloak (Norway)

George Webbe Dasent. *Popular Tales from the Norse*. Edinburgh: n.p. 1888. Translated from Peter Christen Asbjörnsen and Jörgen Möe, *Norske Folke-eventyr*.

Peter Christen Asbjörnsen (1812-85), a zoologist by profession, began collecting folktales in his native Norway in 1837, assisted by his friend, the poet Jörgen Möe (1813-82). They published their tales beginning in 1842 in a series of books. From their collection come such modern favorites as "The Three Billy Goats Gruff."

"Katie Woodencloak" is a variant of tale type 510B (*The Dress of Sun, Moon, and Stars*) but it begins and ends like tale type 510A (*Cinderella*). Such a mix is not uncommon and demonstrates that tale types are merely approximate categories of tale plots. Storytellers have a wide repertoire of characters and episodes from which to create tales, guided by their and their audience's tastes.

It is an interesting and not uncommon bit of fairy tale logic that Katie Woodencloak's disobedience is also her salvation. Against the bull's orders, she plucks leaves of copper and silver and an apple of gold. This results in the death of the bull, yet these very objects enable her to achieve her goal of marrying the prince.

The Wonderful Birch (Finland)

Andrew Lang. *The Red Fairy Book*. London: Longmans, Green, 1890.

Lang's version was translated from Eero Salmelainen's *Tales and Fables of the Finns*. I have added details from the original, as summarized in Marian Roalfe Cox's *Cinderella*, which seem to have been censored by Lang (for instance, "horse-dropping" in Salmelainen has become a "piece of dirt" in Lang's version). See the following notes to the Icelandic "Mjadveig, Daughter of Mani," for information about the Scandinavian troll tradition.

Mjadveig, Daughter of Mani (Iceland)

Jon Arnason. *Icelandic Legends*. Translated by George E.J. Powell and Eirikr Magnusson. Second series. London: Longmans, Green, and Co., 1866.

Jon Arnason (1819-88) was a librarian who, inspired by the work of Jacob and Wilhelm Grimm, collected the folktales of his native Iceland. He had many contacts throughout Iceland who sent him texts of local folktales. Arnason himself was not a tale collector, and the collecting methods of his associates are not known. The word Mani in the Icelandic language is used in myth to refer to the moon, and the word Mjadveig means mead, the intoxicating drink made from honey.

The trolls of Icelandic tradition resemble those of other Scandinavian countries. Female trolls, like the stepmother and stepsister in this tale, were believed to be able to take on human form, and to abduct human men who would then become trolls themselves unless they escaped quickly. In Scandinavian tales and legends, trolls and other supernatural creatures were imagined living inside rocks.

Little Rag Girl (Republic of Georgia)

Marjory Wardrop, translator. *Georgian Folk Tales*. London: David Nutt, 1894. Original title: *Khalkhuri Zghaprebi*, edited by M. Agrniashvili. Tiflis: Georgian Folklore Society, 1891.

The tale of a starved and persecuted girl helped by a cow or a goat that magically produces food from its ear or horn has been widely collected in the Middle East and southeastern Europe. Among the agricultural people of this region, it was usual at the time this tale was collected, and for centuries before, for a girl to be given an animal to mind and a spinning task when she was around the age of seven.

The dropped spindle that leads to the underworld realm of the dead is a motif common to this and other Eurasian folktales, for example, tale type 480, *The Kind and Unkind Girls*.

Vasilisa the Beautiful (Russia)

Post Wheeler. *Russian Wonder Tales*. New York: Century, 1912.

Post Wheeler, translator of this tale, was Chargé d'Affaires at the American Embassy in St. Petersburg, Russia. Although he does not cite exact sources, it seems logical to assume that his tales were taken from the massive collection of Russian folklorist Aleksandr Afanasiev, which were published in eight volumes from 1855-66.

Central to this Russian Cinderella tale is the heroine's stay at the little house in the woods, home of the inimitable Baba Yaga. Baba Yaga appears in many Russian fairy tales and is no mere generic witch, that is to say, she is not simply malevolent. She is both a frightening cannibal and a powerful potential ally. Scholars have likened her to the forces of nature; given her control over day and night, this seems quite obvious. She travels about in a mortar, propelled by a pestle, sweeping away her tracks with a broom. Like the giant in "Jack and the Beanstalk," she has a highly developed sense of smell and can instantly sniff out human—in this case Russian—children.

Baba Yaga lives in a house in a clearing in the woods, surrounded by a fence made of human bones. The little house stands up on chicken legs and turns around when Baba Yaga addresses it by its name, Izbushka. Baba Yaga is described as having one leg of bone and teeth of iron. In some tales, it is said that her body fills the entire house, and this image suggests an association with a corpse in a coffin. In fact, small houses for the dead, partially underground and with a window, were built in parts of Russia. The heroine of the Georgian tale "Little Rag Girl" also visited a strange, possibly dead, woman in an underground house.

Vasilisa is a good example of a fairy tale heroine who acts, rather than reacts. Her self-control at Baba Yaga's house helps win her her freedom from the stepfamily; later, her mastery of the needle arts wins her a royal husband. She is called Vasilisa the Beautiful, but it is her other qualities that enable her to change her life.

For a Jungian analysis of this tale, see Marie-Louise von Franz's "The Beautiful Wassilissa," in her *Problems of the Feminine in Fairytales*, reprinted in *Cinderella: A Folklore Casebook*, edited by Alan Dundes.

The Little Red Fish and the Clog of Gold (Iraq)

Inea Bushnaq. *Arab Folktales*. New York: Pantheon, 1986.

The translator and editor of this tale does not cite an exact source, saying only that she gathered the tales through library research, always looking for good storytelling style. This tale's teller is quite engaging, often addressing the audience, and employing proverbs and sayings to advance the plot and comment upon the events. The collection *Arab Folktales* includes an introduction describing the many different types of storytelling occasions in the Moslem world.

Although the heroine of this tale attends a festive event, a bride's henna, she does not actually meet the prince there. The event serves only for her to put on her beautiful clothes and to lose a shoe which will be found by the prince, recalling the centuries-earlier Egyptian account of Rhodopis.

The "henna" is a women's ritual that is part of preparations for an Islamic wedding. As part of the event, the future bride's hands and feet are painted with henna, a plant dye. This painting is still a part of Islamic weddings and was described to me recently by a young Pakistani-American woman, who came to class with intricate designs all over her hands. She and her friends had painted their own hands at another woman's pre-wedding festivities.

Nomi and the Magic Fish (South Africa: Zulu)

Phumla M'bane. *Nomi and the Magic Fish: A Story from Africa*. Illustrated by Carole Bayard. New York: Doubleday, 1972.

Phumla M'bane, a young woman living in Cape Province, South Africa, was fifteen years old when she wrote down this story in 1969.

Though her native language was Xhosa, she wrote the story in English, and it was subsequently published as a children's picture book.

Despite extensive collecting of folktales in Africa, very few tales like Cinderella have been recorded. In his article, "Cinderella in Africa" (published in the *Journal of the Folklore Institute* in 1972 and reprinted in *Cinderella: A Folklore Casebook*, edited by Alan Dundes), folklorist William Bascom discusses other African narratives that have been classified as Cinderella tales. A Nigerian storyteller told me that the European Cinderella tale was antithetical to his own storytelling tradition, because no good person would ever find happiness by marrying a stranger.

How the Cowherd Found a Bride (India)

Cecil Henry Bompas. *Folklore of the Santal Parganas*. London: David Nutt, 1909.

I have combined parts of two very similar tales in this collection, using the beginning of the tale "The Grateful Cow" as a prelude to the tale "How the Cowherd Found a Bride." The latter tale is much more richly detailed than the former, but it lacks the element of initial villainy in the former, which allies it more clearly with tales of the Cinderella type.

Like many nineteenth-century folklore collectors, Bompas was a colonial civil servant. The area of the Santal Parganas was a British administrative district in Bengal. A hundred years ago, when this tale was collected, *goalas*, or cowherds, formed the most numerous caste in this part of India. Compare this tale to European tales such as "Aschenputtel" using the visual image complex of tree-dead mother-animal-gifts.

The Invisible One (Native American: Micmac)

Charles G. Leland. *The Algonquin Legends of New England: Myths and Folklore of the Micmac, Passamaquoddy, and Penobscot Tribes*. Boston: Houghton Mifflin, 1884.

Charles Leland believed that this tale was an adaptation of a French-Canadian Cinderella story, or possibly even "borrowed" from early Norse explorers of the area (probably because the wooden dress motif is like that in the Norwegian tale, "Katie Woodencloak"). Early European and American folklore collectors seem not to have considered the possibility that Europeans might themselves have borrowed the plots and motifs of folktales from other cultures, such as those of Native Americans.

Poor Turkey Girl (Native American: Zuñi)

Frank Hamilton Cushing. *Zuñi Folk Tales*. New York: G.P. Putnam's, 1901.

I have taken the liberty of shortening Cushing's version a bit, for it seems overweighted with verbose similes that slow down the action of the tale, while adding little for the modern reader. Frank Hamilton Cushing worked for the United States Government's Bureau of Ethnology and lived at Zuñi from 1879-84. He was especially interested in collecting Zuñi folktales.

Folklorist Stith Thompson included this tale in his anthology, *Tales of the North American Indians*, placing it in the section entitled "Tales Borrowed from Europeans." Although the tale of the "Poor Turkey Girl" does resemble the European Cinderella, it is strikingly different, and it would be difficult to prove that it was indeed borrowed, though the Zuñi had had contact with Europeans since the sixteenth century. Other versions of the story of the turkey girl have been recorded at Zuñi more recently, and these later versions are far shorter than Cushings, and bear much less resemblance to the European Cinderella. (See Dennis Tedlock, *Finding the Center*, and The Zuñi people, *The Zuñis: Self-Portrayals*.)

Turkeys, which figure in many of European Cinderella tales (see "Peu d'Anisso" and "Little Rag Girl" in this collection) are native to the Americas. The birds were introduced in Europe by the Spanish, but became established there so quickly that the Pilgrims brought them *back* to America when they arrived at Plymouth.

Cushing himself gathered evidence of how quickly a tale could be appropriated and adapted from one culture to another. In the summer of 1886, he was translating a Zuñi storytelling session to an English-speaking audience when he was unexpectedly called upon to tell a story himself. He responded with the Italian folktale, "The Cock and the Hen," a short cumulative tale. About a year later, Cushing was surprised to hear one of the Zuñi storytellers who had been present retell "The Cock and the Hen." The plot of "The Cock and the Hen" was still recognizable, but the storyteller had greatly expanded the images of the story and the interactions between characters. (See Alan Dundes, *The Study of Folklore*, pp. 269-76, for texts of the two tellings of "The Cock and the Hen.")

Ashpet (United States: Appalachia)

Richard Chase. *Grandfather Tales*. Boston: Houghton Mifflin, 1948.

Richard Chase (1904-88) was both a folklorist and a storyteller who collected Appalachian versions of European folktales in the mountain regions of Virginia and North Carolina. "Ashpet" was told to him by Mrs. Nancy Shores of Wise County, Virginia. The Hairy Man is a figure of Southern U.S. folklore, similar to a troll, ogre, or giant in European folktales. Compare the Hairy Man's spot of vulnerability to that of the whale in "Fair, Brown, and Trembling."

Chase describes his collecting methods in the introduction and notes to this volume and its companion, *Jack Tales*:

> I have taken a free hand in the re-telling. I have put each tale together from different versions, and from my own experience in telling them.

Chase states that in the case of Ashpet he invented the magic washing of the pots and pans and that the request of the old woman to the three girls had originally been that they pick lice from her hair. Delousing one's family members and close friends was once a basic part of good manners in human societies; in adaptations of folktales

for children—or for modern audiences in general—this is usually changed to hair-combing.

Benizara and Kakezara (Japan)

Keiko Seki. *Folktales of Japan*. Translated by Robert J. Adams. Chicago: University of Chicago Press, 1963.

The teller of this tale was Hana Watanabe, the subject of the translator Robert Adams' 1972 doctoral dissertation, "The Social Identity of a Japanese Storyteller." In this fascinating work, Adams describes how Mrs. Watanabe taught herself to read when she was in her sixties, after going deaf, so that, by reading, she would be able to learn more stories to tell.

According to Adams' notes to this story, Benizara's poem is not only more beautiful than Kakesara's, it also follows the rules of the *Waka* or *Tanka* poetic form, which has a 5-7-5-7-7 syllable count. The line-for-line translation reads,

Bon zara y	*Try, plate, oh!*
sara chuu yami ni	*plate on mountain*
	over
yuki furite	*snow falls*
yuki o ne toshite	*snow as root using*
sodatsu matsu ka na	*growing pine it*
	seems.

Kakezara's poem, in addition to being rather insensitive, is in poor poetic form.

According to twentieth-century collecting efforts, it appears that Cinderella tales are widely known and told in Japan. Folklorist Kenichi Mizusawa recorded nearly a hundred in the Echigo district alone.

Maria (Philippines)

Fletcher Gardner. "Filipino (Tagalog) Versions of Cinderella," *Journal of American Folklore* XIX (October-December, 1906).

I have combined parts of two similar tales, both collected in Mindoro, the Philippines, in the Tagalog language in 1903 by Fletcher Gardner. One storyteller was a young man named Cornelio, the other, a woman of about sixty, whose name is not given. The two stories are similar, and each has confusing sections that can be cleared up by reference to the other.

Gardner describes his method of collecting tales:

> The story was taken down by my usual method of listening attentively to the tale in Tagalog, and then at once writing it out in English, from memory, and having this story retold, with the translation at hand, to detect inaccuracies.

Gardner speculates that the tale came to the Philippines through Spanish conquerors; if so, it has been delightfully adapted to include local plants and animals. The tale resembles many European folktales in which the heroine is "marked" with a star or the like on her brow; typically, the evil (step)sister(s) are also marked, but with something disgusting such as a horn (see "Little Rag Girl" in this volume), or a donkey's tail, that cannot be removed. The golden bell in "Maria" somehow does not seem a suitably harsh punishment for the sister, nor a fitting contrast to Maria's jewel. For other Filipino oral variants of this tale, see Don V. Hart and Harriet C. Hart's article, "Cinderella in the Eastern Bisayas" (*Journal of American Folklore* 79, 1966).

The Story of Tam and Cam (Vietnam)

A. Landes. *Contes et legendes annamites*. Saigon: Imprimerie Coloniale, 1886. Translation by Judy Sierra.

Landes was an administrator of native affairs in the French colonial government of Vietnam (then known as Indochina), as well as an amateur collector of folktales. According to the introduction to his collection, Landes employed native translators to collect and transcribe tales exactly as they were told by local storytellers. Landes identifies the species of the fish and bird in this tale as *Gobius biocellatus* and *Ixos analis*, respectively.

The story of Tam and Cam differs from most other Cinderella tales in that the heroine is killed, then successively reincarnated in the form of animals and plants, and finally emerges from a fruit as an even more radiant version of herself. See "The Magic Birch" in this volume and "Cinderella" in Wolfram Eberhard's *Folktales of China* for other examples of shape-changing heroines.

Essays, Activities, and Resources

About Cinderella

The story of Cinderella, best known as a children's story by the French writer Charles Perrault, "Cendrillon, ou la petite pantoufle de verre" (1697), enjoys an enduring popularity in Europe and in parts of the world settled by Europeans. The animated film, *Cinderella*, by Walt Disney (1950) is based on the Perrault telling. Although these versions have preserved the tale in print and on film and videotape, other forms of the tale exist in the oral and written traditions of many parts of the world. Almost all tell the story of a young woman persecuted by her family who receives magical help from unusual sources, so that her true worth can be known by a potential husband of higher rank. (Some male Cinderella tales exist also; see "Billy Beg and the Bull" and "How the Cow-Herd Found a Bride" in this collection.) Certain images recur in Cinderella stories, but always in surprising combinations and permutations. The core images include association of the heroine with hearth and ashes; help from the dead mother; gift-giving tree; helpful animal; food magically produced by animal; magic tree; clothing produced from remains of dead animal; impossible tasks accomplished with the help of animals or strange old woman; impossibly beautiful and impossibly ugly garments provided by father; threefold visit to a dance or church with threefold flight; proof of identity through shoe, ring, or other item of adornment; prince takes the wrong bride; marriage.

What Is a Cinderella Story?

The existence of this group of similar tales has fascinated students of folklore for over a hundred years. The publication of German folktales from the oral tradition by Jacob and Wilhelm Grimm (the first volume of the first edition of their *Kinder- und Hausmärchen* appeared in 1812) inspired folktale collecting activities all across Europe and then throughout the world. As more and more oral tellings were recorded, it became apparent that certain folktale characters, epi-sodes, and plots were indeed international and existed in many places and in many languages.

Folklorists who compared folk narratives from different cultures discerned certain categories of tales, each category consisting of many versions that shared important similarities. The term "tale type" came to be used to designate a basic recognizable story line or plot; "variants" are localized or regional ways of telling a certain tale type; a "version" designates one actual telling, written or oral, of a tale. The Folklore Society of Britain commissioned Marian Roalfe Cox to investigate all known Cinderella stories, and the results of her work were published in 1893 as *Cinderella. Three Hundred and Forty-Five Variants of Cinderella, Catskin, and Cap o' Rushes, Abstracted and Tabulated*. Cox drew her tales not only from published collections, but also from the unpublished folklore archives of many countries. She classified the tales of the persecuted heroine into five main types:

Type A. Cinderella (Ill-treated heroine. Recognition by means of shoe.)

Type B. Cat-skin (Unnatural father. Heroine flight.)

Type C. Cap o' Rushes (King Lear judgment. Outcast heroine.)

Type D. Indeterminate

Type E. Hero Tales

Among these tales, she noted the following sorts of "common incidents," which were widely distributed among tales of this type: ill-treatment of heroine, help at grave, dead mother's help, helpful animal, revivified bones, magic dresses, recognition by means of shoe or ring, substituted bride, happy marriage. Such "common incidents," and many, many more—usually not limited to any one specific tale or tale type—would later be given the name "motif" by folklorists. See Stith Thompson's *Motif Index of Folk Literature* for a comprehensive catalog and classification of these.

Finnish scholar Antti Aarne, in his tale type index (later revised by American folklorist Stith Thompson and published as *The Types of the Folktale*) attempted to classify all the folktales of Europe, India, and areas settled by Europeans into basic types. Aarne and Thompson defined Cinderella tales as those having a sequence of five basic incidents: persecuted heroine, magic help, meeting with prince, proof of identity, and marriage with prince. (They also included a sixth element, "value of salt," which is confusing because it applies only to the "Cap o' Rushes" type of tale.) Stories belonging to Aarne and Thompson's three main Cinderella tale-types, 510A, *Cinderella*; 510B, *The Dress of Gold, of Silver, and of Stars*; and 511, *One-eye, Two-eyes, Three-eyes*, actualize this sequence of episodes in different ways. According to this classification system, the heroine of 510A is persecuted by female relatives, receives aid from her dead mother, meets the prince at a ball or at church, and is recognized by a slipper test. The heroine of 510B is persecuted by her father, receives dresses from her father, meets the prince at a place of employment as a servant, meets him also at church or at a ball, and is recognized by means of a shoe or a ring. The heroine of 511 is persecuted by female relatives, receives help from an old woman and/or an animal, and is spied upon by her sisters. A treasure-producing tree springs up from the helpful animal's entrails, and the heroine then proves her worth to a visiting prince by picking the fruit of the tree.

These simplified plot outlines break down as categories as soon as they are applied to more than one tale. (Try, for example, to classify "Katie Woodencloak" according to these tale types.) Although these tale types describe the basic plots of some European Cinderella tales, the oral tale as a real-world phenomenon is marvellously fluid and resists rigid scientific categorization. While those familiar with one variant of Cinderella can intuitively identify other, similar tales, the tale remains much more than a plot with interchangeable, culture-specific details. Thus, while the concept of tale type is useful in beginning to think about the variation and stability of traditional narrative, it is only a guide.

Cinderella as a Fairy Tale

It is important to situate the European versions of Cinderella in the tradition of the fairy tale—also called magic tale or wonder tale. The most obvious characteristics of this subspecies of the folktale are the appearance of magic elements, and a setting in a world in which, at first glance, anything can happen: in particular, poor girls marry princes and poor boys marry princesses. Researchers have found that these tales of magic have strict rules as to what can occur, and how, and what types of characters take part in the stories.

The Russian folklorist Vladimir Propp worked out a set of rules of the Russian fairy tale in his *Morphology of the Folk Tale*, first published in 1928. These rules, though, do not explain the workings of the heroine tale, such as Cinderella, but rather the hero tale (and, more specifically, the Russian hero tale). Still, Propp's findings shed light on the observable fact that the lines between tale types are blurred, and that episodes associated with one tale type will show up unexpectedly in another. The European fairy tales seem to be constructed from a common set of building blocks and are composed according to an inner logic by which they move from a serious family problem to a series of fantastic adventures to a marriage or similar form of "happily ever after" at the end. Within these rules, the individual storyteller takes a more creative role in the telling than early folklorists realized.

Cinderella in Literature

The first Cinderella story to be written down, so far as is known, was the story of the girl Yeh-hsien, which appeared in a ninth-century Chinese manuscript. The first European Cinderella tale published, though it never became widely known, was "Of a Young Girl Nicknamed 'Ass Hide' and How She Got Married with the Help of Little Ants," in *Les Nouvelles Recreations et Joyeux Devis*, by Bonaventure des Périers (1558). "La Gatta Cenerentola," ("The Cat Cinderella") was one of the stories included by Giambattista Basile in his *Pentamerone* (1634-36). Basile's tale has a convoluted plot that is hard to follow, and I have not included it in this volume. It can be found in Basile's work, as the "sixth diversion of the first day," and is reprinted in Alan Dundes' *Cinderella: A Folklore Casebook* (Garland, 1982).

Charles Perrault's "Cinderella, or the Little Glass Slipper," published with seven other tales from the oral tradition in his *Histoires ou contes du temps passé* (1697), remains the best-known of the literary Cinderella tales. It has truly defined what Europeans and Americans (and, since the Disney film, virtually everyone) think of as Cinderella.

The Cinderella versions published prior to Marian Roalfe Cox's 1893 study scarcely revealed the variety of the tale in oral tradition. And yet, written tradition has profoundly influenced oral tradition. Many folklorists have encountered illiterate storytellers who sought out literate neighbors to read them books of folktales, so that they could expand their repertoires.

The Origins of Cinderella

Inherent in the concept of tale types and variants, as formulated by folklorists a century ago, was the idea that there was once a pure, original tale, which was changed and corrupted through the oral narrative process. Scholars set about compiling and analyzing all known versions of a tale type in order to reconstruct that original tale and decide precisely where and when it originated. Such attempts may seem futile today, but serious scholars devoted their lives to such studies even though, unlike archaeologists, they had no tangible physical remains from the past to help them in their quest. Anna Birgitta Rooth, in her 1951 study, *The Cinderella Cycle*, attempted to discern whether type 510A, 510B, or 511 was the original Cinderella, and to show how the tale spread. She proposed that the very first form of the tale was 511, "One-eyes, Two-eyes, Three-eyes," and that it originated in Asia and changed as it spread to Europe. Though it may one day be possible to know more about the origins of this and other tale types, the arguments of Rooth and others are not convincing, and folklorists have abandoned the quest for origins in favor of the study of living traditions.

Is Cinderella a Worldwide Phenomenon?

When nonfolklorists read of the existence of 345, or 700, or more Cinderella tales, they often imagine these stories equally dispersed among the peoples and geographic regions of the globe. First, the amazing "number" of variants needs to be demystified. Folktales vary widely, not only from culture to culture, but from teller to teller within the same culture, and even from telling to telling by the same person. Such is the nature of the oral tradition that oral narratives are not memorized and recited word-for-word, but reconstructed in each telling from an outline, or a set of intuitive rules of storymaking. Thus, a large number of versions, that is, different tellings, of Cinderella could conceivably be collected in just one culture area. And despite the fact that African and Native American tales resembling Cinderella tales have been recorded, these are very few and far between and do not represent the most important tale plots or themes of any group in these areas. As an oral traditional tale, Cinderella seems to be most widespread among the people of Europe, the Middle East, and Asia.

Magic, Metaphor, and Meaning

More fascinating than the question of where and when certain tales originated is that of their meaning. Tales like Cinderella are filled with extraordinary creatures and magical happenings that transcend everyday reality. How can these elements be explained? Some scholars seek the meaning of fairy tale magic in ritual. Religious historian Mircea Eliade, for example, thought that the European fairy tale was the literary equivalent of the initiation rituals of puberty practiced in early Western and contemporary non-Western societies. For him, the action of the fairy tale, which portrays its heroine's or hero's journey from parental home to marriage by way of a magical and often frightening otherworld, mirrored the ritual journey taken by initiates in many tribal groups.

Also seeking the meaning of Cinderella in ritual, French folklorist Paul Saintyves claimed that the tale of Cinderella originated in the European folk festival of Carnaval in the month of February, a celebration of spring and fertility, and a time of betrothal for young men and women. A masked stepmother figure in this ritual procession represented the old year, and the two evil stepsisters the two months of the new year preceding spring. The figure of the "fiancee of ashes" in the festival, whom Saintyves equated with Cinderella, represented the spring of the new year.

According to many psychologists, the magical content of folktales can be explained by the workings of the unconscious mind. Tales such as Cinderella could be psychologically true, though not literally true, having a metaphorical or symbolic relationship to human life, particularly emotions. For Freudian psychoanalyst Bruno Bettelheim, Cinderella represents a child's perception of normal family events. Young children, according to Bettelheim, are not tolerant of ambiguity in adults, so when the mother begins to demand that the formerly coddled "baby" begin to do housework, she may, indeed, seem like an evil stepmother to the child. The fairy tale allows the child to feel and express anger toward the real mother, and is a safe way of discharging otherwise intolerable feelings. Non-Freudian psychoanalytic interpretations exist also; Marie-Louise von Franz, a student of Carl Jung, has written extensively on the interpretation of fairy tales.

Still other, mythological interpretations have been suggested, identifying fairy tale characters with the sun, the moon, and other forces of nature. The potential for interpretation is endless. In fact, fairy tales seem to *demand* explanation. We sense that they are charged with hidden meaning, and contemporary works of interpretation such as Bettelheim's *The Uses of Enchantment* are widely read by adults.

Is Cinderella Dangerous?

Ever since fairy tales were first written down, and categorized as children's stories, there have been attempts to censor their contents. References to sex and other taboo bodily functions have been almost completely eliminated from tales in children's books. For instance, adults quibble over the "correct" or "original" ending of "Little Red Riding Hood"—did the girl perish inside the wolf, or was she rescued by the woodsman? Both endings are literary creations. Few modern readers would recognize the nearly universal ending of the oral tale, in which Red Riding Hood liberates her-

self. After getting in bed with the wolf, she realizes his evil intentions and, in order to force him to let her escape, says she needs to go outside to relieve herself. Likewise, Cinderella tales such as Perrault's "Peau d'Ane" (tale type 510B), in which the heroine's father wants to marry her after the death of his wife, have been largely censored in English-speaking countries. Apparently such a desire is considered unspeakable, or at least unprintable.

Many parents and teachers fear that the violent elements of fairy tales will frighten children, an attitude Bruno Bettelheim tried to counter in *The Uses of Enchantment*, proposing that fairy tales are actually therapeutic and help assuage a child's fears by resolving them in fictional form.

In the 1970s, feminist writers began to attack the heroine tales, and Cinderella in particular, as bad role models for young girls. There is certainly truth in this, especially if the tales are accepted literally. Fairy tales originated in societies in which a woman's possible roles were very strictly limited. Careers were not an alternative to marriage. In the past twenty years, efforts have been made to identify and publish folk and fairy tales with active heroines, and to produce modern fairy tales that show a young girl having as wide a field of action as the male fairy tale hero. There are actually many traditional tales with active and resourceful heroines, including some Cinderella tales. These were not, however, among the most frequently published in the U.S., though feminist collections published in the 1970s and 1980s have helped change this. Modern, "remedial" fairy tales such as Jay Williams' *The Practical Princess* have failed to capture children's imaginations, while others like Robert Munsch's *The Paper Bag Princess* are appreciated mainly by adults and by children who already know the traditional fairy tales. These retellings criticize, but do not replace, traditional tales, which have a much stronger appeal to children.

For me, the mystery about Cinderella is not its origin, but its overwhelming claim on childrens' imaginations, particularly girls' imaginations, today. Interested adults can never hope to restrict the access of children to Cinderella and other fairy tales in their mass media incarnations. Reading and talking about many versions can help both adults and children clarify the power and personal meanings of the story.

Activities

The following activities are designed for children and adolescents ages nine through fourteen. They have two purposes: first, to expand children's understanding of folklore and particularly the way in which folklore can vary yet remain constant; and second, to use children's familiarity with the Cinderella tale as a strong and natural starting point for projects in writing, drama, and comparative folklore and literature. I worked extensively as an artist-in-the schools, and I confess a deep dislike of detailed and logical lesson plans. I feel that they encourage simplistic thinking and inhibit creative discoveries. The following are basic outlines of activities that I have found successful in classrooms. Instructions are addressed to students, with hints for teachers given in introductions and notes.

Comparative Folklore

1. The Oral Tradition: Use the following questions to initiate an exploration of how oral tradition changes, yet remains the same. There is no one "correct" version of a folktale—or a jump-rope rhyme.

   Do you know a jump-rope rhyme about Cinderella? Write down the words you know. Compare your version with others. In cases where words, names of people, actions, etc., are different, do the different items form categories (that is, are the *differences* alike)?

   Compare your Cinderella rhymes to those collected in Australia by Ian Turner, published in his book, *Cinderella Dressed in Yella*.

   (Note: Girls usually know more jump-rope rhymes than boys. It will probably be best to have students work on this project in mixed-gender groups of three to four.)

2. Folk rituals: Using the following questions, collect and compare "marriage divination rituals." Today, these are usually performed "just for fun," but you will be surprised how many different small rituals your students know. A

discussion can relate folk rituals to folktales—both are fun, neither are true. Make particular note of any rituals you collect which, like the French tradition below, have elements in common with the Cinderella story.

   Do you know any ways to find out the name of the person you're going to marry? Some people say that if you put a piece of wedding cake under your pillow (well-wrapped, of course) that you will dream of the person you're going to marry. In Ireland many years ago, young women would take a tray, put a layer of sand in the bottom, and place a snail on the sand. The snail's sticky trail would spell out the name of their future husband. And in France, girls would throw ashes on their clothes; if they went to bed without speaking a single word, they would dream, so it was said, of their future husband. Have you heard of or seen any other ways of telling who someone will marry?

   (Note: Remembering folklore often takes time, from a few minutes to a few days. Allow time for this activity to percolate.)

Comparison of Folktale Variants

The comparison of different versions of a tale, such as Cinderella, from different cultures is often suggested as a teaching method. Comparing Cinderella tales has a built-in advantage for teachers in upper elementary through high school, because it utilizes a basic story line that is familiar to nearly all students, even those who are recent immigrants, or whose families do not read. Even knowledge of the "Disney version" can be used as a starting point for the comparison of tales' similarities and differences.

Be aware that this activity must be process-oriented, and that even among scholars, there are no agreed upon "right answers" as to how and why folktale variants resemble each other. Folktales shouldn't be used, except very cautiously, as windows into other cultures. For example, it is easy to understand why the Filipino heroine, Maria, has a crocodile helper, and why her magic tree is a grapefruit—the answer is found in natural history. But there is no accepted method of using culture to explain the strange and magical elements of folktales. In her study of the relationship between Zuñi folktales and society, anthropologist Ruth Benedict found that the tales sometimes mirrored, yet often contradicted cultural practices and beliefs.

The following activities are open-ended. I have suggested tales and themes for comparison that I think will lead to interesting discussions or writing projects. They will encourage children to think about folktales in the same way that folklorists do. I have included the folklorist's perspective in teachers' notes, but these are not necessarily the "right answers." Students (and teachers) may offer other equally valid conclusions and insights.

1. Often, folktales have what are called conventional openings and closings. We expect English-language fairy tales to begin with the words, "Once upon a time," and end with the words, "and they lived happily ever after." Look for conventional openings and closings among the Cinderella tales in this book. Can you see any patterns in the way different storytellers open and close their tales? Do they make sense?

   (Note: Conventional openings and closings mark the tale as fiction. An opening like "once upon a time" cues the listener that what is about to be told is untrue, or not entirely true, as the Georgian opening of "Little Rag Girl"—"There was and there was not. . ."—so aptly suggests. Conventional closings seem rather abrupt to modern readers, but for the audience of an oral tale, action is everything. When a story is over, it's over, and the quicker the better. The most satisfying conventional endings return the listener to the everyday world, like Rod Serling relinquishing control of the television at the end of each episode of *Twilight Zone*.)

2. A charm is a rhyme that is supposed to have magical power. "Rain, rain, go away, come again some other day" is a charm we use in the United States. Look at the rhymes and verses in the Cinderella tales in this book (if the tale was not originally told in English, and that includes all the tales given here except "Ashpet" and "Cap o' Rushes," some of the poetry has been lost in the translation). Which rhymes are used to make magical things happen? In what other ways are rhymes used in the stories? Which is your favorite?

   (Note: It's easy to scan the stories for rhymes because they are centered in the text and set in italic type.)

3. Look at two or more Cinderella tales in this book, and compare the animals and the roles they play. Suggested pairings: "Maria" and "Little Rag Girl"; "Cinderella" and "Poor Turkey Girl"; "Nomi and the Magic Fish" and "Yeh-hsien"; "Billy Beg and the Bull" and "Katie Woodencloak."

4. In several tales, a strange woman helps the heroine. Compare the helper in "Cinderella," "Little Rag Girl," "Vasilisa the Beautiful," and "Ashpet." Are these women good or evil? Why, or why not?

   (Note: This activity is intended to initiate a discussion of the differences between appearance and reality. It goes without saying that fairy tales do not go over well with fundamentalist Christians, who interpret non-Biblical magic as exclusively evil.)

5. Many fairy tales in the oral tradition tell of a second misfortune that happens after the wedding of the heroine. In Cinderella stories the stepmother and stepsister may pretend to be friendly while they plan to do away with her. Compare the second test in the following pairs of tales:

   "Mjadveig, Daughter of Mani" and "Tam and Cam."

   "Fair, Brown, and Trembling" and "Ashpet."

   Write a second episode for the Perrault or Disney version of Cinderella. See how many characters from the story you can include in this new episode.

Comparison of Modern Versions of Cinderella

1. Watch the video of Walt Disney's *Cinderella*, and then look at *Cinderella* from the Faerie Tale Theater series. How are the same characters portrayed differently in the two versions? Which do you like best, and why?

   Watch Tom Davenport's film, "Ashpet" (Davenport Films, 1989; available on video). This film is set in Appalachia during World War II. Compare it to the Faerie Tale Theater version, which is also live action and portrays the characters as psychologically complex human beings.

2. Look at and compare these five picture book adaptations of Perrault's Cinderella. They are very different, yet all are considered excellent examples of picture book art.

   Brown, Marcia, reteller and illustrator. *Cinderella.* New York: Macmillan, 1954.

   Erlich, Amy, reteller. *Cinderella.* Illus. by Susan Jeffers. New York: Dial, 1985.

   Galdone, Paul, reteller and illustrator. *Cinderella.* New York: McGraw-Hill, 1978.

   Karlin, Barbara, reteller. *Cinderella.* Illus. by James Marshall. Boston: Little, Brown, 1989.

   Perrault, Charles. *Cinderella; or, The Little Glass Slipper.* Illus. by Errol Le Cain. New York: Faber & Faber, 1972.

   Rank them from one to five, beginning with the one you like best. Have a class or group discussion of likes and dislikes. Did you make decisions based on the kind of art you like, or on how well the pictures tell the story, or both?

   How are the illustrations in these books different from those used in the Walt Disney animated film *Cinderella*?

   Some people think that fairy tales like Cinderella shouldn't be illustrated at all, so that listeners or readers can imagine their own scenes and characters. Do you agree or disagree?

(Note: Other picture book versions of this and other Cinderella tales are listed in the next section.)

Dramatics

The following are some suggestions for informal classroom dramatics.

1. Choose one of the tales in this book, and try to imagine how and where it might have been told three hundred or five hundred years ago. Choose one of the stories in this book, and have someone read it aloud several times, perhaps over a period of several days.

   Stories were often told as everyone performed boring or repetitious chores, such as spinning and carding wool. Choose a more familiar boring task that can be passed from person to person as you sit in a circle. Possible tasks include shelling peas or peanuts in a bowl, polishing a shoe, or untangling yarn or string. Pass the role of storyteller around as you pass the task around. Each person tells as much or as little of the story as he or she wishes, then passes the work—and the story—along to the next person. See if you can pace yourselves so that the very last person ends the story.

   (Note: This activity can be lots of fun. Darkening the room helps reduce tension, and remember, word-for-word memorization is *not* storytelling. With a small amount of practice, most groups can pace a story so it ends when the task reaches the last group member.)

2. Divide one of the stories in this book into scenes, and choose groups to act them out in creative dramatics.

   Tales that lend themselves well to this activity are "Cinderella"; "Little One-eye, Little Two-Eyes, and Little Three-Eyes"; "The Wonderful Birch"; "Vasilisa the Beautiful"; "Nomi and the Magic Fish"; "How the Cow-herd Found a Bride"; and "Benizara and Kakezara."

The following is an example of how a story can be divided into scenes for dramatization. Each scene can have a completely new cast, and the roles that participants may take in each scene should be flexible, and decided by the group (including roles of animals, trees, plants, magical objects, and onlookers who comment on the scene).

Vasilisa the Beautiful

Scene one:	Deathbed scene with mother
Players:	Vasilisa, mother
Scene two:	Father takes a new wife
Players:	Father, stepmother, stepsisters, Vasilisa, doll
Scene three:	Baba Yaga's house
Players:	Vasilisa, Baba Yaga, three horsemen, magic hands, doll
Scene four:	Return to the stepmother's house
Players:	Vasilisa, doll, skull, stepmother, stepsisters

These scenes do not make a seamless whole—if all or several are acted out, narration will be needed to link them together.

(Note: This is an ideal way to involve an entire classroom in interpreting a tale. Allow time for the groups to work and plan together, using mime and suggestion in lieu of costumes and props. Be very firm on this point, because props and costumes inevitably become more important to the players than actions and emotions, and the drama becomes tedious.)

Creative Writing

I believe that folktales are the ideal basis for creative writing because they inspire young writers to reinterpret and elaborate on known scenarios. Cinderella and kindred tales have basic plot structures that are well-known and spare young writers the difficult task of inventing their own story lines.

1. Rewrite Perrault's Cinderella, but reverse the gender of the characters. Cinderella is now a boy (give him a name) with a wicked stepfather and cruel stepbrothers. Did you have trouble switching the roles of girls and boys, fathers and mothers?

2. The character of Cinderella has been criticized for being too nice and too meek, for accepting injustice and waiting patiently for her prince.

Can you imagine Perrault's Cinderella acting differently? Try writing a Cinderella story with a heroine who acts in a different way.

3. Invent a modern-day Cinderella story that takes place in your town. Write the story only up to the point where the evil characters leave the hero or heroine alone at home, while they go to some very special event.

Now switch! Trade papers, so that another writer finishes your story.

(Note: It is usually best to outlaw personal names in this activity, for obvious reasons. Be sure that writers take plenty of time to read the first half of their new story so that the ending will make sense. Conclude this activity by reading the stories aloud.)

Illustrated Picture Book Versions of Cinderella

Like the other well-known fairy tales that make up the cultural heritage of American childhood, Cinderella has been published many times and in many ways, including picture book format. At this writing, 45 picture books entitled "Cinderella" are in print, including several based on the Disney movie and novelties such as "pop-up" books. Almost all of these Cinderellas are translations or reworkings of Charles Perrault's classic French tale, *Cendrillon, ou la petite pantoufle de verre*, first published in 1697. Picture book versions of "Aschenputtel," from the collection of Jacob and Wilhelm Grimm, may also be given the title "Cinderella," which has confused reviewers not familiar with that tale. In addition, one can find several picture book versions from other cultures, usually bearing the announcement that they are Cinderella stories.

The contemporary picture book has a fairly conventional format: most picture books are 32 pages in length—25 to 28 pages of text plus title page, dedication page, etc. The page dimension is usually eight by ten inches or larger. It is characteristic of the picture book that its illustrations are at least as important as the text. The best picture book illustrations extend or complement the text, carrying a narrative content of their own, and suggesting further interpretations and meanings. Many contemporary picture books, such as Maurice Sendak's *Where the Wild Things Are*, have a text written expressly for the picture book format. This is obviously not true of older tales such as Cinderella. When these tales are published in picture book format, the balance and rhythm of text and illustration of which the medium is capable is often not achieved. Picture book versions of Cinderella may simply be illustrated storybooks.

Some writers believe that illustration, particularly the large proportion of illustrations in relation to text required by a picture book format, is antithetical to the proper appreciation of the fairy tale. Bruno Bettelheim, in *The Uses of Enchant-ment*, claimed that fairy tales should not be illustrated at all. An illustrator's ideas would interfere with the child's therapeutic identification with the heroine or hero.

Notwithstanding the advice of this respected expert, picture book editions of fairy tales continue to be published at an astonishing rate, and it seems that every illustrator must try a hand at the classic tales. Familiar titles guarantee bookstore sales, and illustrators receive a larger share of royalties when they work with older, public domain texts, rather than recent, copyrighted work.

The least successful illustrators of Cinderella follow Disney in their stereotypically romantic presentation of the human drama, at the expense of the tale's other possibilities, including Perrault's sly humor. Choices of what to illustrate become overworked clichés, such as the transformation of mice to horses, or lizards to lackeys, shown as a series of time-lapse images. The most successful picture books give the reader images upon which to project their imaginations, rather than the frozen fashion drawings of, say, Diane Goode. Marcia Brown's illustrations for the Perrault version are pastel, dreamy, and stylized—suggesting, but not defining the events of the story. Like those of Ed Young for the Chinese Cinderella tale *Yeh-Shen*, they are artistically conceived, yet hazy and imprecise, allowing young viewers to participate with the illustrator in visualizing the text. The illustrations of Errol Le Cain for a translation of Perrault, and of James Marshall for the nicely abridged text of Barbara Karlin, are outstanding renderings of the humor of the tale.

The following is a bibliography of picture book Cinderellas that are widely available either in bookstores or in library collections. I have not listed any works based on Walt Disney's animated film. Perhaps because these works are guaranteed a market, very little care goes into the preparation of the text or the coordination of text with images lifted from the film.

Charles Perrault's Cinderella

Marcia Brown, reteller and illustrator. *Cinderella*. New York: Macmillan, 1954.

Amy Erlich, reteller. *Cinderella*. Illus. by Susan Jeffers. New York: Dial, 1985.

Fiona French, illustrator. *Cinderella*. Oxford: Oxford University Press, 1988.

Paul Galdone, reteller and illustrator. *Cinderella*. New York: McGraw-Hill, 1978.

Diane Goode, translator and illustrator. *Cinderella*. New York: Knopf, 1988.

Barbara Karlin, reteller. *Cinderella*. Illus. by James Marshall. Boston: Little, Brown, 1989.

Hilary Knight, reteller and illustrator. *Cinderella*. New York: Random, 1982.

Nola Langer, reteller and illustrator. *Cinderella*. New York: Scholastic, 1972.

Charles Perrault. *Cinderella; or, The Little Glass Slipper*. Illus. by Errol Le Cain. New York: Faber & Faber, 1972.

The Grimms' "Allerleirauh"

Jacob and Wilhelm Grimm. *Many Furs: A Grimm's Fairy Tale*. Illus. by Jacqueline I. Sage. Millbrae, CA: Celestial Arts, 1981.

Charlotte Huck, reteller. *Princess Furball*. Illus. by Anita Lobel. New York: Greenwillow, 1989.

Joseph Jacobs' "Tattercoats"

Joseph Jacobs, editor. *Tattercoats*. Illus. by Margot Tomes. New York: G.P. Putnam's, 1989.

Flora Annie Steel, reteller. *Tattercoats: An Old English Tale*. Illus. by Diane Goode. Scarsdale, NY: Bradbury Press, 1976.

Afanasiev's "Vasilisa the Beautiful"

Thomas P. Whitney, translator. *Vasilisa the Beautiful*. Illus. by Nonny Hogrogian. New York: Macmillan, 1970.

Elizabeth Winthrop, adapter. *Vasilissa the Beautiful*. Illus. by Alexander Koshkin. New York: HarperCollins, 1991.

Other Cinderella Variants

Edward B. Adams, editor. *Korean Cinderella*. Illus. by Dong Ho Choi. Rutland VT: Tuttle, 1982. (Bilingual text)

Nonny Hogrogian, adapter and illustrator. *Cinderella*. New York: Greenwillow, 1981. (Grimms' "Aschenputtel")

William Hooks, adapter. *Moss Gown*. Illus. by Donald Carrick. New York: Clarion, 1987. (A version from the Southern U.S.)

Ai-Ling Louie. *Yeh-Shen: A Cinderella Story from China*. Illus. by Ed Young. New York: Putnam, 1988.

Updated Retellings and Parodies

Cole, Babette. *Prince Cinders*. New York: Putnam's, 1987. (Gender role reversal)

Farjeon, Eleanor. *The Glass Slipper*. New York: Viking, 1955. (Novel-length retelling)

Myers, Bernice. *Sidney Rella and the Glass Sneaker*. New York: Macmillan, 1985. (Gender role reversal)

Shorto, Russell. *Cinderella and Cinderella's Stepsister*. Illus. by T. Lewis. Carol Publishing Group, 1990. (Told from Cinderella's *and* stepsisters' points of view)

A Guide to Tale Variants in Collections

The following is a bibliography of versions of Cinderella *not* included in this book, which can be found in collections for children and adults, and which are either currently in print or available in many public and academic libraries. Based on my experience as a folklorist and a storyteller, I have excluded certain versions that I consider too heavily rewritten, particularly those published in children's collections. Therefore, certain tales which are classified as Cinderella stories (in Mary Huse Eastman's *Index to Fairy Tales* and its supplements for example) have not been included. All tales in this bibliography from children's collections are marked with an asterisk(*). Tales that are obviously exact or near reproductions of the same written original are grouped together. Indications of national, geographic, or ethnic origin of the tales appear as given in the source.

Europe

"Askenbasken, Who Became Queen." In *The Cinderella Story*, edited by Neil Philip. New York: Viking, 1989, pp. 52-57. (Denmark)

"Ashy Pelt." In *The Cinderella Story*, edited by Neil Philip. New York: Viking, 1989, pp. 58-59. (Ireland)

"The Black Cat." In *The Cinderella Story*, edited by Neil Philip. New York: Viking, 1989, pp. 122-36. (France)

Compare to *"The Enchanted Black Cat," in *Wonder Tales of Cats and Dogs*, edited by Frances Carpenter (Garden City: Doubleday, 1955), pp. 222-34, for an example of the way in which folktales from the oral tradition are censored and rewritten for children.

"The Bracket Bull." In *The Cinderella Story*, edited by Neil Philip. New York: Viking, 1989, pp. 95-104. (Ireland)

"Burenushka, the Little Red Cow." In *Russian Fairy Tales*, collected by Alexander Afanasiev. New York: Pantheon, 1945, pp. 146-50; in *The Cinderella Story*, edited by Neil Philip. New York: Viking, 1989, pp. 36-39. (Russia)

*"Catskin." In *More English Fairy Tales*, edited by Joseph Jacobs. New York: Putnam's, 1898, pp. 204-10. (England)

*"Cenerentola." In *Old Neapolitan Fairy Tales*, retold by Rose Laura Mincielli. New York: Knopf, 1963, pp. 24-34. (Italy: from Basile, Giambattista. *Il Pentamerone*.)

"Cinderella." In *Folktales around the World*, edited by Richard Dorson. Chicago: University of Chicago Press, 1975, pp. 57-59; in *Folktales of France*, edited by Genevieve Massignon. Chicago: University of Chicago Press, pp. 147-49. (France)

"Cinderella in Tuscany." In *Folklore by the Fireside: Text and Context of the Tuscan Veglia*, by Alessandro Falassi. Austin: University of Texas Press, 1980, pp. 55-67; in *The Cinderella Story*, edited by Neil Philip. New York: Viking, 1989, pp. 150-60. (Italy).

"Donkey Skin." In *Folklore by the Fireside: Text and Context of the Tuscan Veglia*, by Alessandro Falassi. Austin: University of Texas Press, 1980, pp. 42-45. (Italy)

"Donkey Skin." In *Perrault's Complete Fairy Tales*, by Charles Perrault. Translated by A.E. Johnson et al. New York: Dodd, 1961, pp. 92-99. (France)

"Fair Maria Wood." In *Italian Popular Tales*, edited by Thomas Frederick Crane. Boston: Houghton, Mifflin, 1885, pp. 48-53. (Italy)

"The Flying Princess." In *Modern Greek Folktales*, edited by R.M. Dawkins. London: Clarendon Press, 1953, pp. 255-58. (Greece)

*"Khavroshechka." In *Baba Yaga's Geese, and Other Russian Stories*, translated and adapted by Bonnie Grey. Bloomington: Indiana University Press, 1973, pp. 109-13. (Russia)

*"Liisa and the Prince." In *Scandinavian Folk and Fairy Tales*, edited by Claire Booss. New York: Avenel, 1984, pp. 573-79; in *Tales from A Finnish Tupa*, edited by James Bowman and Margery Bianco. Whitman, 1936, pp. 187-98. (Finland)

*"Little Bull-Calf." In *More English Fairy Tales*, edited by Joseph Jacobs. London: David Nutt, 1894, pp. 186-91. (England)

"Mossycoat." In *Folktales of England*, edited by Katherine Briggs and Ruth Tongue. Chicago: University of Chicago Press, 1965, pp. 16-26; in *Book of British Fairy Tales*, edited by Alan Garner. New York: Delacourt, 1984, pp. 47-57. (England)

"Mossycoat." In *The Cinderella Story*, edited by Neil Philip. New York: Viking, 1989, pp. 63-69. (England: Gypsy)

*"Olga and the Brown Cow." In *Tales from Central Russia*, edited by James Riordan. Middlesex: Kestrel, 1976, pp. 238-40. (Russia)

"One-Eye, Two-Eyes, Three-Eyes." In *Folklore by the Fireside: Text and Context in the Tuscan Veglia*, by Alessandro Falassi. Austin: University of Texas Press, 1980, p. 34. (Italy)

*"One Eye, Two Eyes, Three Eyes." In *Tit for Tat*, edited by Mae Durham. New York: Harcourt, Brace, 1967, pp. 24-29. (Latvia)

*"Preziosa, the She-Bear." In *Old Neapolitan Fairy Tales*, retold by Rose Laura Mincielli. New York: Knopf, 1963, pp. 54-63. (Italy: from Basile, Giambattista. *Il Pentamerone*.)

*"Rushen Coatie." In *More English Folk and Fairy Tales*, edited by Joseph Jacobs. London: David Nutt, 1894. pp. 163-68. (Scotland)

"La Sendraoeula." In *The Cinderella Story*, edited by Neil Philip. New York: Viking, 1989, pp. 74-78. (Italy)

*"Tattercoats." In *More English Folk and Fairy Tales*, edited by Joseph Jacobs. London: David Nutt, 1894. pp. 76-82. (England)

"The Travellers' Cinderella." In *The Cinderella Story*, edited by Neil Philip. New York: Viking, 1989, pp. 161-74. (Scotland)

Middle East

"An Armenian Cinderella." In *100 Armenian Tales*, edited by Susie Hoogasian Villa. Detroit: Wayne State Univ. Press, 1966, pp. 240-44; in *The Cinderella Story*, edited by Neil Philip. New York: Viking, 1989, pp. 46-51. (Armenia)

*"Gulaida." In *The Bird of the Golden Feather and Other Arabic Folktales*, translated by Gertrude Mittleman. New York: Roy, 1969, pp. 30-42. (No specific country given)

"Moon Brow." Mills, Margaret A. "A Cinderella Variant in the Context of a Muslim Women's Ritual." In *Cinderella: A Casebook*, edited by Alan Dundes. New York: Garland, 1982, pp. 185-88. (Iran)

"The Princess in the Suit of Leather." In *Arab Folktales*, edited and translated by Inea Bushnaq. New York: Pantheon, 1986. pp. 193-200. (Egypt)

"The Poor Girl and Her Cow." In *The Cinderella Story*, edited by Neil Philip. New York: Viking, 1989, pp. 40-45. (Iraq)

Asia

"Andé-Andé Lumut." Danandjaja, James. "A Javanese Cinderella Tale and Its Pedagogical Value." In *Cinderela: A Casebook*, edited by Alan Dundes. New York: Garland, 1982, pp. 170-74. (Indonesia)

"The Boy and His Stepmother." In *The Cinderella Story*, edited by Neil Philip. New York: Viking, 1989, pp. 87-90. (India)

"Cinderella." In *Folktales of China*, edited by Wolfram Eberhard. Chicago: University of Chicago Press, 1965, pp. 156-61. (China)

"Kajong and Haloek." In *The Cinderella Story*, edited by Neil Philip. New York: Viking, 1989, pp. 21-31. (Vietnam)

Africa

*"The Stepchild and the Fruit Trees." In *Singing Tales of Africa*, retold by Adjai Robinson. New York: Scribner's, 1974, pp. 24-33. (Sierra Leone/Nigeria)

The Americas

*"Catskins." In *Grandfather Tales*, by Richard Chase. Houghton Mifflin, 1948, pp. 106-14. (United States)

"Dona Labismina." In *The Cinderella Story*, edited by Neil Philip. New York: Viking, 1989, pp. 70-73; *"Why the Sea Moans." In *Perhaps and Perchance*, compiled by Laura E. Cathon. New York: Abingdon, 1962, pp. 217-27. (Brazil)

"The Golden Filly Chest." In *Tales from the Cloud Walking Country*, by Marie Campbell. Bloomington: Indiana University Press, 1958, pp. 196-98. (United States)

*"Like Meat Loves Salt." In *Grandfather Tales*, by Richard Chase. Boston: Houghton, Mifflin, 1948, pp. 124-29. (United States)

"Little Cat Skin." In *Tales from the Cloud Walking Country*, by Marie Campbell. Bloomington: Indiana University Press, 1958, pp. 82-83. (United States)

"The Little Stick Figure." In *Folktales of Chile*, edited by Yolando Pino-Saavedra. Chicago: University of Chicago Press, 1967, pp. 99-103. (Chile)

"Maria Cinderella." In *Folktales of Chile*, edited by Yolando Pino-Saavedra. Chicago: University of Chicago Press, 1967, pp. 89-99. (Chile)

"Princess That Wore a Rabbit-Skin Dress." In *Tales from the Cloud Walking Country*, by Marie Campbell.

Bloomington: Indiana University Press, 1958, pp. 161-63. (United States)

"Queen with the Golden Hair." In *Tales from the Cloud Walking Country*, by Marie Campbell. Bloomington: Indiana University Press, 1958, pp. 30-31. (United States)

"Rushycoat and the King's Son." In *The Cinderella Story*, edited by Neil Philip. New York: Viking, 1989, pp. 144-49. (United States)

"A Silver Tree with Golden Apples." In *Tales from the Cloud Walking Country*, by Marie Campbell. Bloomington: Indiana University Press, 1958, pp. 43-45. (United States)

*"Turkey Girl." In *Old Father Storyteller*, by Pablita Velarde. Santa Fe, NM: Clear Light, 1989, pp. 31-37. (Native American: Pueblo)

Recommended Further Readings about Cinderella Tales

Bettelheim, Bruno. *The Uses of Enchantment: The Meaning and Importance of Fairy Tales*. New York: Vintage Books, 1977.

Includes a psychoanalytical study of Cinderella (pp. 236-77).

Bottigheimer, Ruth. *Grimms' Bad Girls and Bold Boys*. New Haven: Yale University Press, 1987.

See particularly Bottigheimer's analysis of the changes the Grimms made in the Cinderella tale, "Aschenputtel," from the first to the final edition (pp. 57-70).

Cox, Marian Roalfe. *Cinderella. Three Hundred and Forty-Five Variants of Cinderella, Catskin, and Cap o' Rushes, Abstracted and Tabulated*. London: David Nutt, 1893.

Cox includes synopses of all 345 variants, including many which have never been translated into English.

Dundes, Alan, ed. *Cinderella: A Folklore Casebook*. New York: Garland, 1982.

Especially recommended in this volume are "Cinderella," by W.R.S. Ralston; "Cinderella in China," by R.D. Jameson; "The Beautiful Wassilissa," by Marie-Louise von Franz; and "America's Cinderella," by Jane Yolen.

Falassi, Alessandro. *Folklore by the Fireside: Text and Context of the Tuscan Veglia*. Austin: University of Texas Press, 1980.

Falassi documents a session in which several storytellers compete to tell rival versions of Cinderella (pp. 54-68).

Holbek, Bengt. *The Interpretation of Fairy Tales*. Folklore Fellows Communications no. 239. Helsinki: Academia Scientiarum Fennica, 1987.

Especially interesting are Holbek's analyses of Cinderella tales told by Danish peasant narrators in the nineteenth century, and recorded by Evald Tang Christiansen (pp. 552-58).

Philip, Neil. ed. *The Cinderella Story*. New York: Viking, 1989.

An anthology of twenty versions, six of which are also included in the present volume; many are fragmentary or in heavy dialect.

Taggart, James M. *Enchanted Maidens: Gender Relations in Spanish Folktales of Courtship and Marriage*. Princeton: Princeton University Press, 1990.

Taggart presents Cinderella tales he recorded in Cáceres, Spain, in the 1980s, along with sociological analysis, in the chapter, "Cinderella" (pp. 93-115).

Whalley, Irene. "The Cinderella Story, 1724-1919." In *The Signal Approach to Children's Books*, edited by Nancy Chambers. Scarecrow: 1981, 140-55.

A survey of early illustrated editions of Perrault's tale.

Works Consulted

Aarne, Antti, and Stith Thompson. *The Types of the Folktale.* 2nd rev. ed. Folklore Fellows Communications no. 184. Helsinki: Academia Scientiarum Fennica, 1961.

Adams, Richard. "The Social Identity of a Japanese Storyteller." Ph.D. diss. Indiana University, 1972.

Afanasiev, Aleksandr. *Russian Fairy Tales.* Trans. by Norbert Guterman. New York: Pantheon, 1945.

Angelopoulou, Anna. "Fuseau des cendres." *Cahiers de Littérature Orale* 25 (1989), 71-96.

Arnason, Jon. *Icelandic Legends.* Trans. by George J. Powell and Eirikr Magnússon. Second series. London: Longmans, Green, 1866.

Ashliman, D.L. *A Guide to Folktales in the English Language.* Westport, CT: Greenwood Press, 1987.

Belmont, Nicole. "De Hestia a Peau d'Ane: Le destin de Cendrillon." *Cahiers de Littérature Orale* 25 (1989), 11-32.

Benedict, Ruth. *Zuñi Mythology.* New York: Columbia University Press, 1935.

Bettelheim, Bruno. *The Uses of Enchantment: The Meaning and Importance of Fairy Tales.* New York: Vintage Books, 1977.

Bompas, Cecil Henry. *Folklore of the Santal Parganas.* London: David Nutt, 1909.

Booss, Claire, ed. *Scandinavian Folk and Fairy Tales.* New York: Avenel, 1984.

Bottigheimer, Ruth. *Grimms' Bad Girls and Bold Boys.* New Haven: Yale University Press, 1987.

———, ed. *Fairy Tales And Society: Illusion, Allusion and Paradigm.* Philadelphia: University of Pennsylvania Press, 1986.

Briggs, Katherine. *An Encyclopedia of Fairies.* New York: Pantheon, 1976.

Bushnaq, Inea, trans. *Arab Folktales.* New York: Pantheon, 1986.

Chase, Richard. *The Jack Tales.* Boston: Houghton, Mifflin, 1943.

———. *Grandfather Tales.* Boston: Houghton, Mifflin, 1948.

Climo, Shirley. *The Egyptian Cinderella.* New York: Crowell, 1989.

Cox, Marian Roalfe. *Cinderella. Three Hundred and Forty-Five Variants of Cinderella, Catskin, and Cap o' Rushes, Abstracted and Tabulated.* London: David Nutt, 1893

Crane, Thomas Frederick. *Italian Popular Tales.* Boston: Houghton, Mifflin, 1885.

Curtin, Jeremiah. *Myths and Folk Tales of Ireland.* Boston: Houghton, Mifflin, 1890.

Cushing, Frank Hamilton. *Zuñi Folk Tales.* New York: G.P. Putnam's, 1901.

Darnton, Robert. *The Great Cat Massacre and Other Episodes in French Cultural History.* New York: Vintage, 1984.

Dasent, George Webbe. *Popular Tales from the Norse.* 3rd edition. Edinburgh: David Douglas, 1888.

Dégh, Linda. *Folktales and Society: Story-telling in a Hungarian Peasant Community.* Bloomington: Indiana University Press, 1969. Revised 1989.

Delargy, James. "The Gaelic Story-Teller." *Proceedings of the British Academy,* 1945, pp. 177-221.

Djeribi, Muriel. "De la nourriture aux parures." *Cahiers de Littérature Orale* 25 (1989), 55-70.

Dundes, Alan, ed. *Cinderella: A Folklore Casebook.* New York: Garland, 1982.

———, ed. *The Study of Folklore.* Englewood Cliffs, NJ: Prentice-Hall, 1965.

Eastman, Mary Huse. *Index to Fairy Tales, Myths and Legends.* 2nd ed. Boston: F.W. Faxon, 1926.

———. *Index to Fairy Tales, Myths and Legends: First Supplement.* Boston: F.W. Faxon, 1937.

———. *Index to Fairy Tales, Myths and Legends: Second Supplement.* Boston: F.W. Faxon, 1952.

Eliade, Mircea. *Rites and Symbols of Initiation.* New York: Harper and Row, 1958.

Ellis, John M. *One Fairy Story Too Many: The Brothers Grimm and Their Tales.* Chicago: University of Chicago Press, 1983.

Falassi, Alessandro. *Folklore by the Fireside: Text and Context of the Tuscan Veglia.* Austin: University of Texas Press, 1980.

Gardner, Fletcher. "Filipino (Tagalog) Versions of Cinderella." *Journal of American Folklore* XIX (October-December, 1906), 265-73.

Holbek, Bengt. *The Interpretation of Fairy Tales.* Folklore Fellows Communications no. 239. Helsinki: Academia Scientiarum Fennica, 1987.

Ireland, Norma O. *Index to Fairy Tales 1949-1972: Including Folklore, Legends and Myths in Collections.* Metuchen, NJ: Scarecrow, 1973.

———. *Index to Fairy Tales 1973-1977: Including Folklore, Legends and Myths in Collections*. Metuchen, NJ: Scarecrow, 1985.

———, and Joseph W Sprung. *Index to Fairy Tales 1978-1986: Including Folklore, Legends and Myths in Collections*. Metuchen, NJ: Scarecrow, 1985.

Jacobs, Joseph. *Celtic Fairy Tales*. London: David Nutt, 1892.

———. *English Fairy Tales*. New York: G.P. Putnam's, 1898.

———. *More English Fairy Tales*. London, David Nutt, 1894.

Landes, A. *Contes et légendes annamites*. Saigon: Imprimerie Coloniale, 1886.

———. *Contes tjames*. Saigon: Imprimerie Coloniale, 1897.

Lang, Andrew. *Red Fairy Book*. London: Longmans, Green, 1890.

———. *Green Fairy Book*. London: Longmans, Green, 1892.

Leland, Charles G. *The Algonquin Legends of New England*. Boston: Houghton, Mifflin, 1884.

Lüthi, Max. *The European Folktale: Form and Nature*. Trans. by John D. Niles. Bloomington: Indiana University Press, 1982.

———. *The Fairytale as Art Form and Portrait of Man*. Trans. by Jon Erickson. Bloomington: Indiana University Press, 1984.

MacDonald, Margaret Read. *The Storytellers' Sourcebook: A Subject, Title, and Motif Index to Folklore Collections for Children*. Detroit: Gale/Neal-Schuman, 1982.

MacManus, Seumas. *In Chimney Corners*. New York: Doubleday, 1899.

Massignon, Genevieve, ed. *Folktales of France*. Chicago: University of Chicago Press, 1968.

McGlathery, James M., ed. *The Brothers Grimm and Folktale*. Urbana: University of Illinois Press, 1991.

Morgan, Jeanne. *Perrault's Morals for Moderns*. New York: Peter Lang, 1985.

Munsch, Robert. *The Paper Bag Princess*. Annick, 1980.

Pedroso, Consiglieri. *Portuguese Folk-tales*. London: The Folk-Lore Society, 1982.

Perrault, Charles. *Contes de Perrault: Fac-similé de l'édition originale de 1695-1697*. Geneva, Switzerland: Slatkine Reprints, 1980.

Philip, Neil, ed. *The Cinderella Story*. New York: Viking, 1989.

Phumla. *Nomi and the Magic Fish*. Illus. by Carole Byard. New York: Doubleday, 1972.

Propp, Vladimir. *Morphology of the Folktale*. 2nd ed. Austin: University of Texas Press, 1968.

———. *Theory and History of Folklore*. Minneapolis: University of Minnesota Press, 1984.

Rooth, Anna Birgitta. *The Cinderella Cycle*. Lund, Sweden: Gleerup, 1951.

Saintyves, Paul. *Les contes de Perrault et les récits paralleles*. Paris: Émile Nourry, 1923.

Seki, Keiko. *Folktales of Japan*. Chicago: University of Chicago Press, 1963.

Simonsen, Michele. *Le conte populaire français*. Paris: Presses Universitaires de France, 1981.

Simpson, Jacqueline. *Icelandic Folktales and Legends*. Berkeley: University of California Press, 1972.

Taggart, James M. *Enchanted Maidens: Gender Relations in Spanish Folktales of Courtship and Marriage*. Princeton: Princeton University Press, 1990.

Tatar, Maria. *The Hard Facts of the Grimms' Fairy Tales*. Princeton: Princeton University Press, 1987.

Tedlock, Dennis. *Finding the Center*. Lincoln: University of Nebraska Press, 1978.

Thompson, Stith. *The Folktale*. Berkeley: University of California Press, 1946.

———. *Motif Index of Folk Literature: A Classification of Narrative Elements in Folk Tales, Ballads, Myths, Fables, Mediaeval Romances, Exempla, Fabliaux, Jest-Books, and Local Legends*. 6 vols. Bloomington: Indiana University Press, 1955-58.

———. *Tales of the North American Indians*. Bloomington: Indiana University Press, 1929.

Ting, Nai-Tung. *The Cinderella Cycle in China and Indo-China*. Folklore Fellows Communications no. 213. Helsinki: Academia Scientiarum Fennica, 1974.

Turner, Ian. *Cinderella Dressed in Yella*. New York: Taplinger, 1972.

Von Franz, Marie-Louise. *Problems of the Feminine in Fairytales*. Dallas, TX: Spring Publications, 1972.

Wardrop, Marjory, translator. *Georgian Folk Tales*. London: David Nutt, 1894.

Weigle, Marta, ed. *Two Guadalupes: Hispanic Legends and Magic Tales from Northern New Mexico*. Santa Fe, NM: Ancient City Press, 1987.

Wheeler, Post, trans. and comp. *Russian Wonder Tales*. New York: Century, 1912.

Williams, Jay. *The Practical Princess*. New York: Parents, 1969.

Zipes, Jack. *The Brothers Grimm: From Enchanted Forests to the Modern World*. New York: Routledge, 1988.

Zuñi people. *The Zuñis: Self-Portrayals*. Trans. by Alvina Quam. Albuquerque: University of New Mexico Press, 1972.

Index

by Janet Perlman